Nonfiction Books for Children

Nonfiction Books for Children
Activities for Thinking, Learning, and Doing

Carol A. Doll
Graduate School of Library and Information Science
University of Washington

1990
TEACHER IDEAS PRESS
A Division of
Libraries Unlimited, Inc.
Englewood, Colorado

TEACHER IDEAS PRESS
A Division of
Libraries Unlimited, Inc.
P.O. Box 6633
Englewood, CO 80155-6633

Library of Congress Cataloging-in-Publication Data

Doll, Carol Ann, 1949-
    Nonfiction books for children : activities for thinking, learning,
and doing / Carol A. Doll.
    x, 117 p. 17x25 cm.
    Includes index.
    ISBN 0-87287-710-8
    1. School libraries--Activity programs.   2. Children's literature-
-Bibliography.   3. Children--Books and reading.   I. Title.
Z675.S3D599   1990
027.8'222--dc20   90-13370
                                                                        CIP

Table of Contents

Introduction

Nonfiction titles have the potential to enhance and enrich classroom instruction in many ways. Many good information books for children are available in school library media centers and public libraries. These books are usually accurate, authoritative, and often fascinating. Because of the age of some collections, currency of some titles could be a problem. However, this can be turned to an advantage if students are led to question and update the material.

This book is intended to give practical guidance in integrating quality nonfiction titles with the elementary school curriculum. All types of information books have been included, and several suggested activities are given in each chapter. While specific titles are used as examples, teachers and media specialists are free to adapt the activities to other books.

Selected information is given in each unit based on a nonfiction title: the bibliographic citation for the book discussed; a brief summary of the book; suggested grade levels, relevant curriculum areas, and objectives; the activity itself, with a listing of materials needed; and additional things to be considered. The teacher or media specialist should read thoroughly the activity and the additional considerations and should examine the book before deciding whether to do the activity with students.

Activity grade levels are generally based on the reading or interest level of the specific book title being discussed. Both individual children and groups of children vary widely in their reading ability. Teachers and media specialists should use their professional judgment in determining whether a specific title or activity is appropriate for a particular child or group of children.

The subject of the book used has, to a certain extent, dictated the related subject areas. School curricula vary widely from district to district. Again, educators should use their professional judgment to select activities appropriate to a given situation.

The activities are designed so students do as much of the work as possible. For example, in a scavenger hunt, students provide the questions and answers to be used. This has two benefits. One, students can learn as much from setting up the questions and answers as they learn by doing the activity itself. And, two, teachers and media specialists will have more time for other duties.

While this book presents units based on fifty-seven specific titles, many more good information books are available. The appendix lists sources that can help in the identification of other books. The school library media specialist also knows both the materials in the school collection and the school curriculum and can provide invaluable assistance to classroom teachers in selecting and using quality nonfiction titles in the classroom. The indexes, both a grade level index and a subject/activity index, will provide additional guidance.

Information Books

An information book is one with good basic content that explores a topic in some depth, with the intent of imparting some understanding to the reader. It is more than just a listing of facts.

Because the intent of these books is to build understanding, they must be well written. As teachers know, student comprehension depends on a logical, clearly explained presentation of the information. Often, the author of an information book is trying to teach without the benefits of personal interaction. This means that the book must be written well enough to "stand alone" so that the reader can comprehend the material by reading it, without questioning the author.

Of course, some authors do a better job of presenting their information than others. In general, successful writers of information books fall into two categories: those who have been trained in a particular discipline, such as astronomy or American history; or those who are professional writers with the skills needed to research and write on many varied topics. Both types of writers can do a very good job.

Information books should be accurate. There is no excuse for including incorrect or misleading information in these books. Currency is another element to consider when judging these titles. To a certain extent, currency depends on the subject of the book. Some areas, such as space flight, change quite rapidly. Older geography books no longer have the correct names for some countries. Other topics are much slower to change, such as books about the American Revolution or George Washington. Also, information titles should be authoritative. The author should have taken the time to research the topic thoroughly, and this background work should provide the basis from which the book is written.

Ideally, these titles should not show bias. Every author brings his or her personal background and beliefs to his or her writing. Often, this enthusiasm is communicated to and intrigues the reader. At the same time, the author has a responsibility to present a balanced discussion or at least acknowledge other points of view. Children's books should not be propaganda. All forms of stereo-typing should be avoided.

Illustrations are often an important part of an information book. They can add to both the understanding and enjoyment of the reader. Illustrations should be captioned and placed in close proximity to the text that discusses or refers to them. A table of contents, glossary, index, and bibliography can be other useful additions.

An information book can be highly specialized (*Uranus* by Branley, p. 5) or more general (*Seeds* by Lauber, p. 8). Any topic can be appropriate. Fascinating information books are available in both school library media centers and public libraries. Some children need a little encouragement to look for them.

Asimov, Isaac. *Words from the Myths.*
Boston: Houghton Mifflin Company, 1961.

SUMMARY: Using Greek mythology as a starting point, Asimov traces the impact of those early myths on the words we use today.

GRADE LEVEL: 5th and 6th grades

CURRICULUM AREA: Language Arts; Social Studies; Semantic Mapping

OBJECTIVES: To increase student knowledge of word origins
To increase student appreciation of Greek myths

ACTIVITY:
Materials: Dictionary, current magazines

1. Briefly discuss the origin of Greek myths. Explain that these myths have even affected our culture today and that the class is going to explore this.

2. Assign students (individually or in groups) to read Greek myths and research a particular character or characters. Suggestions are listed below:

Achilles	Narcissus
Amazons	Orpheus
Aphrodite	Orion
Apollo	Pan
Ares	Pandora
Artemis	Pegasus
Athena	Persephone
Atlas	Pluto
Daphne	Poseidon
Gorgons	Prometheus
Hephaetus	Theseus
Hera	Titan
Heracles	Uranus
Hermes	Zeus
Icarus	

3. Based on their readings, students should begin to create a semantic map. (A general format is given at the end of this unit.) They can fill in the areas for Greek name, major deeds and characteristics.

4. Next have students identify the Roman version of their characters' names and adventures. (Asimov's book can help.) Then they can fill in appropriate blanks on the semantic map.

5. Next, students should check the dictionary for a brief definition of each word listed. They should also note any other forms of the word, filling in the semantic map as they work.

6. Asimov says these words, or derivatives of them, are part of the English language today. Students may be familiar with uses of these words or be able to locate examples of how they are used in current magazines. For example, NASA may use some names in the space program. This information can go on the semantic map.

7. Finally, students can check their entries in Asimov's book and enter the information on the worksheets.

8. After students finish, class discussion can be used to emphasize the way these myths influence the English language. Have students give examples. Did they identify things Asimov missed? Why did he not list those? (The book is over twenty-five years old. Language is still evolving.)

9. Completed maps can be posted in the classroom.

CONSIDERATIONS:
1. This could be an extra-credit activity for gifted students.

2. This could become a contest activity, with teams competing to find the greatest number of words in the magazines or the most new uses that Asimov did not list.

GENERAL SEMANTIC MAP

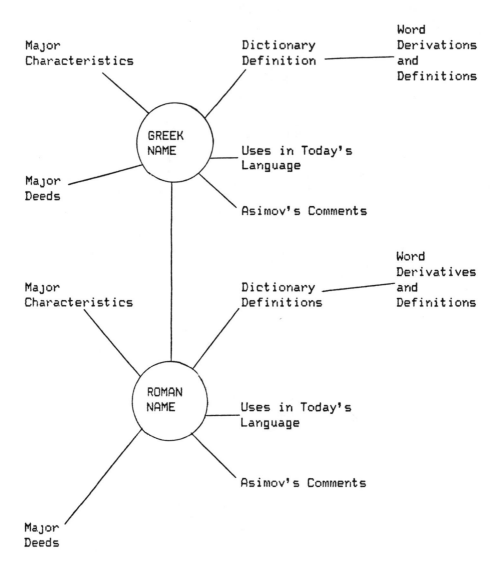

Branley, Franklyn M. *Flash, Crash, Rumble, and Roll.*
New York: Thomas Y. Crowell, 1985.

SUMMARY: Discusses and explains thunderstorms, lightning, and thunder, with added information on safety.

GRADE LEVEL: 1st and 2nd grades

CURRICULUM AREA: Science; Reading; Evaluating Information

OBJECTIVES: To teach students about thunderstorms
To teach students how to keep safe during a thunderstorm
To give students practice in identifying important points

ACTIVITY:
Materials: Blank flash cards, marking pens

1.   Share Branley's book with students. It is probably best to divide the material into several lessons (e.g. thunderstorms, lightning, thunder, safety tips).

2.   Discuss the material covered with the students. Help them identify the most important points.

3.   Divide the class into groups. Each group should make up three sets of questions and answers based on the material covered. Students should make one flash card for each set of questions and answers.

4.   Repeat this procedure for each lesson.

5.   When all the material has been covered, divide class into teams. The flash cards can be used for a "weather bee," patterned after the traditional spelling bee.

CONSIDERATIONS:
1.   It may be a good idea for the teacher to check the flash cards daily to judge quality and correct errors. If desirable, duplicate questions can be eliminated before the final contest.

2.   Branley suggests two activities that could be done in the classroom: using a balloon to make sound waves and counting seconds to estimate the distance of a thunderstorm.

Branley, Franklyn M. *Uranus: The Seventh Planet.*
New York: Thomas Y. Crowell, 1988.

SUMMARY: Branley briefly gives the history of the discovery of Uranus, and then describes what is currently known, incorporating data and pictures from Voyager 2.

GRADE LEVEL: 5th and 6th grades

CURRICULUM AREA: Science; Creative Writing; Applying Information

OBJECTIVES: To teach students about our solar system
To give students a chance to apply creative writing skills
To give students a better understanding of science fiction

ACTIVITY:
1. This unit is designed to be used after students have learned about our solar system.

2. Discuss with students what science fiction is and the role of science in science fiction.

3. Tell students they will become science fiction writers and create a setting based on the information in Branley's book. They will need to consider such things as temperature, atmosphere, light, clouds, rotation, satellites, wind, colors, and so on. Students should create a situation bringing their protagonists into contact with the planet in some manner and for some reason. Setting should be emphasized and it may not be necessary for students to write a complete book or short story.

4. The following brief scenarios may be used to help students get started:

   a. An exploratory, manned spacecraft from earth is approaching Uranus. There is a systems' failure on board. Where should they try to land and what preparations should be made for survival as they await rescue?

   b. Aliens approach Uranus with the intent of colonizing the planet. What must they be like if they consider Uranus as a workable location for a colony? What type of a settlement might they build?

   c. A spaceship from earth is orbiting Uranus. The people are there to "mine" the planet or its moons. How will they deal with climate and other planetary factors? What substance(s) have they come to get? How will they collect it/them?

5. Students may wish to share results with the class or in small groups.

6. Class discussion after students have finished writing can emphasize the connection between science and science fiction. This would also give students an opportunity to share any problems or frustrations caused or emphasized by the need to adhere closely to the known facts while creating the setting.

CONSIDERATIONS:
1. It may be beneficial to have students work in pairs, instead of individually.

2. Any information book about the planets, the sun, or the moon could be used in this way.

Gibbons, Gail. *Fill It Up! All about Service Stations.*
New York: Thomas Y. Crowell, 1985.

SUMMARY: Describes the many activities that can take place in a busy service station that has a tow truck and mechanics on duty.

GRADE LEVEL: Kindergarten through 2nd grade

CURRICULUM AREA: Social Studies; Classification

OBJECTIVES: To show students the range of activities possible in a service station

To show students that this book describes *one* service station and that individual service/gas stations can differ

ACTIVITY:
1. Share Gibbons's book with students.

2. Discuss with students gas stations, service stations, convenience stores, or other places where their parents buy gas. Explore ways these places are similar to and different from each other and from Gibbons's fictional station. For example, what can be bought at a convenience store that cannot be found at a full service station and vice versa? This is a good opportunity for students to compare, contrast, or classify their information about gas stations.

3. Emphasize to students that information in a book is not always exactly like their local situation. Gibbons's station is not "wrong," just different.

4. Have students ask their parents how much they paid per gallon for gas the last time they fueled the car. The students will also need to know what kind of gas was purchased. Talk about why there is a difference in gas prices. (Location, type of place where gas was purchased, or the brand of gas can all be considered.)

CONSIDERATIONS:
1. This activity could be good preparation for or follow-up to a field trip to a local station.

2. Teachers may wish to invite a local station owner to visit the classroom.

3. Have groups of students work together to design their own service stations. Decisions about type, products, services to be offered, and so forth should be based on previous class discussion or library research. Then, each group should advertise their services and prices to the rest of the class. Voting can determine who attracts the most customers.

Lauber, Patricia. *Seeds: Pop! Stick! Glide!*
New York: Crown Publishers, Inc., 1981.

SUMMARY: Lauber discusses the many different ways plant seeds are dispersed. Includes detailed photographs by Jerome Wexler.

GRADE LEVEL: 3rd and 4th grades

CURRICULUM AREA: Science; Classification

OBJECTIVES: To reinforce for students ways in which seeds travel
To give students experience in gathering seeds and determining how they are dispersed

ACTIVITY:

Materials: Chart listing ways seeds travel, magnifying glass, containers and envelopes for seeds, notebook

1. Set up a learning center containing the items listed above.

2. Share all or part of Lauber's book with students and discuss the different ways seeds may travel.

3. Help students to identify characteristics of seeds that indicate how they travel. Discuss how students can apply the characteristics to new seeds. Help students identify what to look at or questions to ask to determine how a seed travels or is carried. A poster or checklist of the points to look at or questions to ask can be placed in the learning center.

4. As a continuing project, have students find seeds and bring them to school. Then they can use the learning center, with Lauber's book for reference, to determine how seeds travel. The containers and envelopes can be used to store the seeds collected so other students can also look at them. The notebook can be used to record: seed number, collector, where seed was found, date brought in to school, how the seed travels, and plant the seed came from.

5. It may be valuable for students to share their work with others in the school. Groups of children could work together to create story posters or bulletin boards for the various types of seeds, emphasizing their characteristics and dispersal method. An opaque projector, cut-out or hand-drawn pictures, or the seeds themselves can be used to illustrate the posters. The results can be displayed in the school library media center, the hallways or somewhere else where other students can see them. Be sure students sign their work.

6. When the learning center is closed, class discussion can be used to review what students learned and the seeds collected.

CONSIDERATIONS:
1. The teacher may wish to bring in "mystery seeds" one at a time for students to look at. Students can use secret ballots to tell what they know or find out about the seed — how it travels, what kind it is, and so on. The teacher could "tell all" on Fridays, including the tally of the secret vote.

2. It would be possible to plant some of the seeds, continuing to study and observe the plants themselves rather than just the seeds.

Perl, Lila. *Don't Sing before Breakfast, Don't Sleep in the Moonlight: Everyday Superstitions and How They Began.* **New York: Houghton Mifflin Company, 1988.**

SUMMARY: A discussion of the origin and meaning of some common superstitions.

GRADE LEVEL: 3rd and 4th grades

CURRICULUM AREA: Social Studies (Customs and Beliefs); Library Skills; Scientific Method; Collecting and Evaluating Information

OBJECTIVES: To increase student awareness of customs and habits
To show students how to use books as information sources, with emphasis on index skills
To have students use scientific method to test a superstition or superstitions

ACTIVITY:
Materials: Worksheets; charts for record keeping

1. Discuss with students habits and customs as patterns of behavior we all follow. Talk about good luck and bad luck. Introduce the idea of superstitions. Briefly show students Perl's book.

2. Have each student write down at least one superstition. Teachers may wish to have students do this at home and bring it to school the next day if they have trouble thinking of one in class.

3. During free time in the classroom, have students use the index in Perl's book to read their comments about their superstitions. Students should then summarize and paraphrase the authors' comments on their worksheets (see the example at the end of this unit). Page numbers consulted in the book should be given by each student.

4. Worksheets can be compiled in a folder or notebook for the whole class to browse in free time.

5. Work with the class to select two or more superstitions to investigate. Devise a technique to test whether or not the superstition is true. For example, to test "If you sing before seven, you'll cry before eleven," the class could be divided into two groups. One would sing when they got up every morning for a week; one group would not sing.

6. Devise a chart to record results of the students who sang for one box, those who didn't for another. Then split the group into those who cried and those who did not.

	Sang before 7:00 a.m.	Didn't sing before 7:00 a.m.
Cried before 11:00 a.m.		
Didn't cry before 11:00 a.m.		

Five sets of boxes would be needed for the week.

7. At the end of the experiment discuss results with students.

CONSIDERATIONS:
1. If students do not know how to use an index, it may be necessary to teach that skill before doing this unit.

2. When selecting a superstition to test, pick one that can be checked easily. For example, it would not be successful to test whether or not broken mirrors bring seven years bad luck.

3. To extend this unit, students may wish to build a notebook of family superstitions by interviewing parents, grandparents, aunts, uncles, other family members, or even neighbors. It could be helpful to note whether the interviewed people believe in the superstitions completely, somewhat, or not at all. In light of the experiments done in class, students could discuss how they feel about the veracity of the superstitions. It would be possible to calculate the percentage of adults who believe in specific superstitions or who are superstitious in general. Students could also make graphs and charts based on their data.

SUPERSTITION WORKSHEET

Name: _____

Superstition: _____

_____

_____

Index pages in Perl's book: _____

Summary of Perl's comments:

_____

_____

_____

_____

_____

_____

_____

_____

_____

_____

_____

_____

_____

_____

_____

_____

_____

_____

Simon, Seymour. *Mars.*
New York: William Morrow and Company, 1987.

SUMMARY: A brief discussion of historical events associated with Mars is followed by factual information about the planet based on data gathered by four Mariner and two Viking spacecraft.

GRADE LEVEL: 4th and 5th grades

CURRICULUM AREA: Science; Critical Thinking; Evaluating Information

OBJECTIVES: To increase student knowledge of the planet Mars
To give students a chance to compare and evaluate old and new information about the planet Mars

ACTIVITY:
Materials: One or more older titles about Mars or the planets in general with specific sections on Mars (e.g., Branley, Franklyn. *The Nine Planets*. New York: Thomas Y. Crowell, 1985; Asimov, Isaac. *Mars*. New York: Follett, 1967; Branley, Franklyn. *A Book of Mars for You*. New York: Thomas Y. Crowell, 1968)

1. To introduce the topic, ask students what they know about the planet Mars.

2. If students don't bring it up, mention and discuss the Mariner and Voyager spacecraft. Ask students what difference these spacecraft could make in our knowledge of Mars.

3. Explain that older books on Mars and Simon's book on Mars are available in the learning center. Students are to:

   a. Identify what the old book(s) say about a topic.

   b. Identify what the newest book says on that same topic.

   c. Determine what differences there may be in the information in the older and newer books. Then students should try to explain why there may or may not be differences. For example, scientists were right before and there has been no change; scientists were guessing before and the new data has proven them right or wrong; or this is totally new information not mentioned in earlier books.

4. Students may pick their own topic, or teachers may wish to assign topics such as: life on Mars, the canals, water/ice, volcanoes, or what causes the red color.

5. Have each student or group of students write a news flash based on their newest information. This news should be appropriate for a radio announcement as if it were "hot off the wire" from NASA.

6. Use the news flashes to make an audiotape so students can listen to each others' work. Use the tape to spark discussion about how and why some information changed and some didn't. Teachers may wish to stop the tape after each announcement or a related group of announcements instead of playing the entire tape at once.

CONSIDERATIONS:
1. Magazine articles based on data from the Mariner or Voyager spacecraft can also provide information and can be used instead of or in addition to Simon's book. The school library media specialist can help in locating such articles.

2. Some schools have older filmstrips about the planets. One on Mars could be used in step 1 to introduce the topic. It could also be used as a source of older information for comparison purposes.

3. This same activity could be done with volcanoes, using the eruption of Mount St. Helens as the latest, newest incident. Possible books to use include:

    Irving, Robert. *Volcanoes and Earthquakes*. New York: Knopf, 1962.

    Lauber, Patricia. *Junior Science Book of Volcanoes*. n.p.: Garrard, 1965.

    _____. *Volcano: The Eruption and Healing of Mount St. Helens*. Scarsdale, N.Y.: Bradbury Press, 1987.

    Poole, Lynn, and Gary Poole. *Volcanoes in Action: Science and Legend*. New York: McGraw-Hill, 1962.

Thomson, Peggy. *Keepers and Creatures at the National Zoo.* New York: Thomas Y. Crowell, 1988.

SUMMARY: A behind the scenes look at the animals and people who care for them at the National Zoo in Washington, D.C.

GRADE LEVEL: 4th through 6th grades

CURRICULUM AREA: Science; Library Skills; Vocational Guidance; Change Based on New Evidence

OBJECTIVES: To better prepare students for a field trip
   To increase student knowledge about some common zoo animals
   To give students practice in finding information about animals
   To give students information about the job of zoo keeper
   To help students understand some of the newer methods of handling animals in zoos and reasons for the changes

ACTIVITY:
1. First, give students a general introduction to the unit. This activity is designed to be used as a part of a field trip.

2. Assign students to investigate specific animals. This may be an individual or a group activity. The appearance, habitat, characteristics, behavior, and special concerns (e.g., whether it is an endangered species) of the animals can be researched. It is better to concentrate on animals that will be seen on the field trip. A suggested list is given below:

bear	giant panda
cobra	gorilla
cuttlefish	pygmy hippopotamus
bat	elephant
lion	red panda
tiger	orangutan
sea lion	sloth
giraffe	golden lion tamarin

3. After the library research is finished, have students consult Thomson's book to research their animal in the zoo.

4. Next, students should investigate older ways of building zoo enclosures and the newer, more environmental housing. For their assigned animal, each group can draw or model the two types of housing. Books, magazines, television programs, or interviews may be helpful sources of information.

5. Students should be able to give some reasons for the change in the ways animals are housed in zoos.

6. Have each group make a brief presentation to the class to share the information they have collected. Drawings and models can be displayed in the classroom or in the school library media center.

7. Students are now ready for the field trip. If a zoo guide or other education personnel from the zoo can accompany students on their tour, it can enhance the experience.

CONSIDERATIONS:
1. The same general technique can work for field trips to museums, bakeries, airports, or similar locations if books can be found that give the needed background information.

2. Students could also investigate the history of zoos and the change in attitude from the days of "bring 'em back alive" and Frank Buck to today's emphasis on saving endangered species.

3. If a field trip is not planned, this could be used as a research project emphasizing library skills.

4. Make sure information is available on the animals selected so students won't become frustrated looking for obscure animals.

Informational Picture Books

By definition, a picture book is one that uses both pictures and text to tell the story or convey the information contained. Neither the text nor the illustrations can stand alone. Instead both work together and are equally important to the contents of the book.

While many picture books are fictional, some are truly *informational* in purpose and therefore fit the scope of this book.

In addition to the usual concerns with currency, accuracy, authority, and author's qualifications, the illustrations and pictures are very important to the information picture book. They should be clear and unambiguous. Since the function of these pictures is to convey information, they must do so. Readers should be able to identify objects in the pictures easily and quickly see the characteristics or relationships being discussed. Any captions should be pertinent and easy to match to the appropriate picture or portion thereof. Pictures without captions should be placed next to the pertinent text so that readers will not become confused.

Nonfiction picture books often contain specialized information in one location that might otherwise be scattered throughout reference tools or more general books in the media center. Aliki's *A Medieval Feast*, for example, gives many details about menus and feasts in the Middle Ages. And, it does so in twenty-eight profusely illustrated pages. Often the nonfiction picture book is a good place to start investigating a topic. The simplified approach can give an uncluttered introduction to the topic, which can then be more fully explored through other sources.

Sometimes this simplified approach can be a weakness in a nonfiction picture book. If the content is oversimplified and vital relationships omitted or obscured, inaccuracies or false impressions can result.

Overall, information picture books have great potential for classroom use. They can provide a good introduction to some topics. Clear pictures can enhance the information. If the teacher is promoting their use and the stigma of "baby books" is removed, some slower students may be able to use them easier than traditional textbooks.

Aliki. *A Medieval Feast.*
New York: Thomas Y. Crowell, 1983.

SUMMARY: When the king announces his upcoming visit, the entire manor is involved in preparing the feast to be held in his honor.

GRADE LEVEL: 5th and 6th grades

CURRICULUM AREA: Social Studies; Creative Writing; Collecting and Using Information

OBJECTIVES: To increase student knowledge of the Middle Ages
To encourage student application of library skills
To provide students an opportunity for creative writing and creative dramatics

ACTIVITY:
Materials: Tape recorder, blank tape

1. Share the book with the class.

2. Explain to students they will be doing a radio interview of people involved in the feast before and possibly during the event.

3. Assign each student a role from the list below. Teachers may wish to omit or combine some parts. Roles are listed in the order they appear in the book.

The King	Beekeeper
The Queen	Miller
Knight	Baker
Squire	Ale and wine maker
Lord of the manor	Dairyman
Lady of the manor	Head cook
Serf	Assistant cook
Ladies who spun thread	Scullion boy
Ladies who wove fabric	Serf who served the table
Serf who cleaned manor	Panter
Serf who set up tents	Ewerer
Serf who fenced field	Trumpeter
Those in hunting party	Bishop
Serf who trained falcons and hawks	Jester
Serf who caught rabbits and birds	Juggler
Serf who went fishing	Minstrel
Gardener	Interviewer

4. Students are to research the role they have been assigned. For example, the student who is the falconer may find out more about falconry, its role in medieval society, and use this information to explain what this job involves, how the falconer feels about the upcoming visit, any problems it causes, and any special opportunities it may present.

5. Once the research is done, have students write questions and answers to show the knowledge gained and show their character's feelings of concern, pride, and anticipation of the upcoming event, as well as the amount of work required to prepare for the visit.

6. Plan for the interviews. Include the order in which characters will speak, the length of each interview, and overall length of the tape.

7. Practice the entire event at least once.

8. Tape the interviews.

CONSIDERATIONS:
1. If the school has a radio program, all or part of this exercise may be broadcast to the school.

2. This could be a good activity to present on parents' night. Parents may wish to have a copy of the tape.

3. It is possible to do a videotape or a play based on this book. In this case be sure to consider costuming and scenery.

Anno, Mitsumasa. *Anno's Alphabet: An Adventure in Imagination.*
New York: Thomas Y. Crowell, 1974.

SUMMARY: Anno's alphabet book uses optical illusions to present the twenty-six letters. One large picture per letter is used as an example, and additional objects in the ornate borders also begin with the letter under consideration.

GRADE LEVEL: 4th through 6th grades

CURRICULUM AREA: Library Skills; Creative Writing; Evaluating and Applying Information

OBJECTIVE: To provide students with a chance to apply dictionary skills and/or library reference skills
To give students a chance to create their own alphabet books

ACTIVITY:

Materials: Multiple copies of Anno's alphabet book (available in paperback)

1. Divide students into groups of two or three. Then divide the groups into sets of two.

2. Assign each pair of groups one letter from Anno's book.

3. Students are to identify as many of the objects as they can that are pictured on the pages and that begin with the relevant letter.

4. Identification should not be written on the book but rather on separate sheets of paper.

5. When students have finished, matched groups should compare answers. The group with the most answers wins. In case of a tie, the group with the lowest search time wins.

6. Discuss with students the objects Anno chose to include in his pictures. Out of all the *A* words available, why did he include anvil, ant, aster, acanthus, and anemone? Were these good choices? Why or why not?

7. Based on this discussion, work with the class to formulate rules for alphabet books. For example, it is best to avoid objects with multiple meanings like bunny, hare, jackrabbit, and rabbit. Also, it is wise to use care in the initial sounds. Words like eye, knife, wheel, shine, stitch, or snow may be inappropriate unless a special "doesn't follow the rules" book is being written. Also, mention there can be three types of alphabet books—potpourri (like Anno's book), related example (e.g., all animals or fruit), or one that tells a story.

8. Have each group of students work together to formulate the rules they will follow and then write an alphabet book. They can illustrate their book with their own pictures, photographs, or pictures cut from old magazines.

9. When the books are done, have students share them with the kindergarten or first grade.

CONSIDERATIONS:

1. In the back of the book Anno lists *some* of the things in his pictures. You may wish to avoid showing this list to students until after the exercise is finished. It may be possible to "seal" this list by wrapping paper or a book cover around the last pages of the book.

2. The procedures used in the library to locate information are probably more important than the number of items found.

3. Because of more obscure terms, it may be better to avoid the letters *U*, *X*, and possibly *E*.

4. Anno's "Traveler" books will also work well for scavenger hunts if students work to identify historical events and people, scenes from literature, famous paintings, etc.

5. When discussing alphabet books, it may be helpful to bring to class a number of alphabet books by other authors to show the potential range of topics and spark student imaginations.

Bare, Colleen Stanley. *Guinea Pigs Don't Read Books.*
New York: Dodd, Mead and Company, 1985.

SUMMARY: Briefly lists things guinea pigs can and cannot do. Most importantly, they can be your friends.

GRADE LEVEL: 1st and 2nd grades

CURRICULUM AREA: Science; Creative Writing; Art

OBJECTIVES: To give students experience in creating a book
To give students a chance to draw or take pictures of an animal
To give students experience in finding facts about an animal

ACTIVITY:
Materials: A three-ring notebook, lined paper for the notebook, drawing paper, crayons

1. Share Bare's book with the class.

2. Tell students that the class as a whole will write and illustrate their own book about an animal.

3. Select the animal to be the subject of the book. A classroom mascot would be a good choice. Also, it would be better if the animal chosen is not too similar to a guinea pig. Fish, hermit crabs, birds, cats, or dogs could work well.

4. Use class discussions to list things the animal can do or cannot do.

5. Reference books in the library can help students identify characteristics of the animal, such as variety in color, number of legs, and so on.

6. Work on the lists and characteristics until at least one item is identified for each student in the class.

7. Have each student then write a sentence about his or her assigned item and draw a picture to illustrate that sentence.

8. All pages are then collected, put into a coherent order, and placed in the notebook.

9. Display the book in the classroom.

CONSIDERATIONS:
1. Teachers may wish to use a camera, either a Polaroid or another easy-to-operate camera, to make color prints. Then photographs could be mounted in the notebook instead of student drawings.

2. Students may wish to practice drawing and sentence writing before making the final copy.

3. The notebook can be a nice display item for parents' night or PTA meetings. Consider having students sign their pages.

4. It would be possible to divide students into groups and have each group make a book. It would probably work better if each group worked on a different animal.

5. An accordian book format could be used instead of a three-ring notebook. This would ensure that each child's work would be seen when the book is on display.

Baskin, Leonard. *Hosie's Alphabet.*
New York: The Viking Press, 1972.

SUMMARY: A remarkable alphabet book featuring colorful animals and insects accompanied by descriptive adjectives in a variety of type styles selected to enhance the mood of words used.

GRADE LEVEL: 3rd through 6th grades

CURRICULUM AREA: Language Arts; Art; Visual Literacy

OBJECTIVES: To give students an opportunity to use color and letter shape creatively to reflect mood
To make students more aware of connotative meanings of words

ACTIVITY:
Materials: Art paper, writing supplies (e.g., marking pens, crayons, paint, caligraphy supplies), old magazines

1. Share Baskin's book with the students. Emphasize his use of letter size, color, and/or shape to enhance the mood.

2. Have students use a similar technique to call attention to the meaning of words they will use to describe a picture cut from an old magazine. Students should work both to select strong, descriptive adjectives and to convey meaning and mood through size, shape, and colors.

3. Let students work on the project.

4. Display the results in the classroom.

CONSIDERATIONS:
1. Students could draw their own pictures instead of using magazines.

2. It would be possible to select a specific theme or topic for students to work on, such as buildings, people, or sports.

3. This activity could be set up in a learning center if it is inconvenient as an activity for the entire class.

Gibbons, Gail. *Weather Forecasting.*
New York: Four Winds Press, 1987.

SUMMARY: A detailed examination of weather forecasters and their work. Includes specific terminology for both weather phenomena and the instruments used to monitor and predict weather conditions.

GRADE LEVEL: 3rd and 4th grades

CURRICULUM AREA: Science; Language Arts; Evaluating Information

OBJECTIVE: To familiarize students with terminology of weather and weather forecasting

ACTIVITY:
Materials: Microcomputer software program that makes crossword puzzles (helpful, but not mandatory)

1.   Introduce students to Gibbons's book.

2.   Set up a learning center in the classroom. Students, either individually or in small groups, are to identify fifteen to twenty important points in Gibbons's book. Then, they are to select a key word and write a clue or definition for the identified points.

3.   These key words and clues/definitions are to be used to create a crossword puzzle. If a microcomputer software program is available to do this, students should follow its instructions. Otherwise, it is possible to create the puzzle with paper and pencil.

4.   For each puzzle, students should turn in a reproducible master (if possible, let students make multiple copies).

5.   A sample list of words and definitions are given below. Italicized words are to be blanks in the puzzle.

   front: line of changing weather between two kinds of air masses

   hurricane: destructive windstorm that comes from the tropics

   radiosonde: sends information back to the weather office from the weather balloon

   cirrus clouds: mean fair weather

   cumulonimbus clouds: mean thunderstorms

   altostratus clouds: mean rain or snow

   cirrostratus clouds: mean a change in weather

   air *mass*: body of air with the same temperature and moisture

   Greenwich: all weather stations are on _____ mean time

high pressure: when air pressure rises

low pressure: when air pressure falls

extended forecast: long-range forecast

tornado: a destructive funnel-shaped cloud

rotating beam *ceilometer*: measures cloud height from the ground

rain *gauge*: measures the amount of rainfall

barometer: measures air pressure

precipitation gauge: indicates the amount of rain or snow

meteorologist: the weather expert

weather *forecaster*: person who predicts the weather

anemometer: measures wind speed

thermometer: measures air temperature

solar instrument: registers minutes of sunshine in a day

wind *vane*: shows wind direction

6. After a period of time (one to two weeks) finish the puzzle-making phase of the learning center activity. Then put out multiple copies of the crossword puzzles for students to solve. Later the answers can be posted.

7. At the conclusion of the unit it may be helpful for students to discuss the techniques used and problems encountered (and solved) in writing their crossword puzzles.

CONSIDERATIONS:
1. Gibbons's book does not have an index or a glossary, so students must read the book to find the main points.

2. This technique could work for any picture book pertinent to classroom studies. However, it works better if the title does not have an index.

3. It is possible to have students work individually or in groups and keep track of the number of puzzles correctly solved, and/or the time taken to fill in the correct answers.

Hoban, Tana. *Look Again.*
New York: Macmillan Publishing Company, Inc., 1971.

SUMMARY: The reader's attention is initially focused on a small area of a black and white photograph. Turning the page reveals the entire familiar picture. For example, stripes become zebras and abstract shapes become the bottom of a turtle. An intriguing venture into visual discrimination and picture reading.

GRADE LEVEL: Kindergarten through 3rd grade

CURRICULUM AREA: Art; Visual Literacy; Reading Readiness

OBJECTIVE: To increase student ability to recognize detail in pictures

ACTIVITY:
Materials: Old magazines with lots of pictures, heavy paper or tagboard (the same size as the sheets of construction paper) with a hole cut in it — one or more per child, scissors, paste, construction paper

1. Share the Hoban book with the children.

2. Explain they will look through the magazines to find pictures to stump their classmates.

3. Pictures should be cut out and pasted on the construction paper so the appropriate portion is seen through the hole in the tagboard. Students may do as many as the teacher feels would be useful, probably three to four.

4. Students will share their results with each other. It is probably best to do this in small groups since masked pictures will probably be small.

CONSIDERATIONS:
1. You may wish to supply students with one cover sheet (with a hole in it) per picture. Taping the two together along one side would allow students to flip the pages, as in the book.

2. This also could be used as a learning center activity. Instructions could be given on audiotape for nonreaders.

3. Third graders could share their masked pictures with kindergarten students.

4. Depending on their ability level, students could vary the size or shape of the hole in the masking sheet to hint at the subject matter. Or, several masking sheets could be used, with each succeeding sheet revealing more of the underlying picture.

5. A video camera could be used to film close-up views of the masked pictures. After a suitable period of time (15 to 20 seconds), the mask could be turned and the full picture revealed. (This would also work well for pictures with multiple masks.) This video could be used with the entire class as the visuals would be easier to see than the smaller pictures. It would even be possible to divide the class into teams and use a spelling-bee format for a contest or game.

Reference Books

Reference books are those titles in the media center that are used primarily as sources of information. Encyclopedias, almanacs, atlases, and biographical dictionaries are examples of reference books.

Reference books are important sources that can be used to quickly check for facts or simple answers. Generally, they do not have the in-depth discussion or specialized scope found in other nonfiction books. Usually reference books do not circulate so they are readily available to those people who come to the media center to look up information or to verify facts.

Reference books should be timely. Often, the type of information in these titles, such as population, crop yields, or the winners of the latest academy awards, changes quickly. Library literature usually recommends that a media center purchase the latest editions of almanacs and yearbooks and that a new edition of other reference titles, including atlases and encyclopedias, be purchased every five years.

It is generally acknowledged that today's students need to learn certain library skills. The ability to use common reference books is one type of library skill that helps to make students independent library users, an important ability in today's world.

Commire, Anne, ed. *Something about the Author: Autobiography Series, 1-7.*
Detroit: Gale Research, 1986- .

SUMMARY: Biographical information on each author or illustrator of books for young people is supplemented by comments made by the author or illustrator. Includes portraits and pictures from the books.

GRADE LEVEL: 5th and 6th grades

CURRICULUM AREA: Language Arts; Critical Thinking

OBJECTIVES: To have students become familiar with at least one author
To give students experience in using *Something about the Author: Autobiography Series*
To give students experience in thinking about and questioning the creative process

ACTIVITY:
Materials: A piece of creative writing

1. Tell students the class will be doing a project on authors. Students may select an author or one may be assigned to each student. The author should be included in *Something about the Author: Autobiography Series*. Some authors and titles are suggested at the end of this unit.

2. Have students read a book by their author.

3. After they read the book, students should think about the writing process: Why did the author write this book? Where might the idea have come from? Is any of it based on the author's real life experiences? How did the author learn about things in the book (e.g., the setting, information about jobs, or what it's like in school)? Was it easy or hard to write this book? Does the author enjoy writing? Have students record their analysis of the creation of their book either in writing or on tape.

4. Students should then use *Something about the Author: Autobiography Series* to find out about their author.

5. Based on the autobiographical information, have students evaluate the earlier analysis of their authors' writing process. Which guesses were correct? Which were wrong? What new insights did the student gain from the autobiographical information? What areas of concern or interest were not addressed? If it were possible, what questions would the student ask the author?

6. Next, have students analyze their own methods of creative writing using one of their own pieces and answering the same questions they asked of their authors' work in step 3. Would they change anything in their previous work? What? How? Why?

7. Finally, have students write a brief essay or make a brief recording detailing how their perception of the creative process has changed as a result of this exercise.

CONSIDERATIONS:
1. Teachers may wish to have students write letters to their authors incorporating the unanswered questions from step 5. If the letters are to be mailed, each student should write a different author and a stamped, self-addressed envelope should be included.

2. Several authors (e.g., Phyllis Naylor, Beverly Cleary, Cynthia Rylant) have published autobiographies if students are interested in pursuing this topic.

3. Marguerite Henry has done a filmstrip on the creative process involved in writing *San Domingo* (*Story of a Book, Second Edition: with Marguerite Henry*. Verdigo City, Pa.: Pied Piper Productions, 1983). If students know the book (a possible read aloud) this exercise could be done as a whole-class discussion, following the steps outlined above and using the filmstrip for autobiographical information. Then students could perform the procedure for individual authors.

4. To update or personalize the author list, quickly scan entries in the available volumes of *Something about the Author: Autobiography Series*. Titles of books written by the authors are italicized. It is relatively easy to skim quickly through the entries and identify relevant titles.

SAMPLE AUTHOR/TITLE LIST

Betsy Byars	*After the Goat Man* (New York: Viking, 1974) *The Pinballs* (New York: Harper, 1977) *The Summer of the Swans* (New York: Viking, 1970)
Scott Corbett	*The Lemonade Trick* (Boston: Little Brown, 1960)
Jean Fritz	*China Homecoming* (New York: Putnam, 1985)
Doris Gates	*Little Vic* (New York: Viking, 1951) *A Morgan for Melinda* (New York: Viking, 1980)
Myra Cohn Livingston	*Whispers and other Poems* (New York: Harcourt, 1958) *Wide Awake and other Poems* (New York: Harcourt, 1959)
Emily Cheney Neville	*It's Like This, Cat* (New York: Harper, 1963) *Berries Goodman* (New York: Harper, 1965)
Marilyn Sacks	*Amy Moves In* (Garden City, N.Y.: Doubleday, 1964)
Pamela L. Travers	*Mary Poppins* (New York: Reynal and Hitchcock, 1934)
Yoshito Uchida	*Journey to Topaz* (New York: Scribner, 1971)

Goode's World Atlas. 12th edition.
Edited by Edward B. Espenshade, Jr. Chicago: Rand McNally and Company, 1964.

SUMMARY: A general atlas of the world, giving political divisions, economic projects, geographical and geologic facts, and other miscellaneous information.

GRADE LEVEL: 4th through 6th grades

CURRICULUM AREA: Social Studies; Library Skills

OBJECTIVE: To give students experience in using an atlas

ACTIVITY:
Materials: Index cards

1. Introduce students to the atlas. Tell them what types of information the atlas contains and how to use it. Teachers may wish to work with the school library media specialist.

2. Each student will write two or three "scavenger hunt" questions using the atlas. Number each question (e.g., Ann will write questions 1 through 3; John will do questions 4 through 6, etc.). One index card will have the question number and the question. A second index card will have the answer, the page number for the answer, the atlas skill involved, and the student name. Students should write questions that emphasize the skills needed to use the atlas.

   For example:

---

1. Which state in the U.S. harvests most of the spring wheat?

---

1. North Dakota
   page 59
   using the index
   Ann Jones

2. What are the latitude and longitude of San Francisco?

2. 37.45N   122.26W
   page 262
   index skills
   Ann Jones

3. Of Karzawa, Japan, or Takayama, Japan, which is at the highest altitude?

3. Takayama
   page 153
   index skills; using relief information
   Ann Jones

3. All cards will be turned in to the teacher. Sort the cards into groups. It may not be necessary to use all the cards.

4. Divide the class into groups. Each group will receive a packet of questions and must use the atlas to answer them. They can write their answers on the question cards, including the page numbers where they found the answers and their names. Cards should be turned in to the teacher with a finish time indicated.

5. Give each team a set of cards other than their own. Have them match their cards with the original answer cards and check any discrepancies. They should tally the number of right answers.

6. The team with the most correct answers in the shortest time wins.

CONSIDERATIONS:
1. Students should not answer their own questions. Teams can exchange their cards with the teacher's extra cards or with each other.

2. Professional judgment should be used to determine how many questions each team should answer.

3. All students should be using the same edition of the atlas.

4. The information in atlases does change. In almost any atlas, especially an older one, some of the information will be outdated. This presents an opportunity for students to compare old and new information, using either different editions of atlases or current news magazines such as *Newsweek* or *Time*. Discuss with students possible reasons for the changes noticed.

The Information Please Almanac, Atlas and Yearbook, 1988. **41st edition.**

Boston: Houghton Mifflin Company, 1988.

SUMMARY: A compilation of facts and general information on a wide variety of topics ranging from astronomy to entertainment to mayors to Nobel prizes to religion to zip codes.

GRADE LEVEL: 5th and 6th grades

CURRICULUM AREA: Library Skills; Evaluating Information

OBJECTIVES: To give students practice in using *The Information Please Almanac*
To give students a chance to compare and evaluate information from various sources

ACTIVITY:

Materials: A variety of reference books (consult with your school library media specialist)

1. Introduce students to *The Information Please Almanac*. Be sure to indicate one purpose of the book is to provide quick access to facts and figures.

2. Discuss with students whether or not they believe the information in this book is accurate and true. (The school library media specialist can help find material about the strengths and weaknesses of almanacs.)

3. Discuss with students whether they believe that information from different sources will always agree. Why or why not?

4. Explain to students they will be using five different sources to look up facts in the following areas:

    a. A famous person. This should be someone, either living or dead, who is well known. Facts students should collect include birth date, when the person died (if applicable), and one or two reasons why the person is famous.

    b. An economic fact. This would include things such as the dollar amount of domestic car sales or median family income. If figures are listed for more than one year, have students note the last three entries with the corresponding dates.

    c. A geographic fact. This will include things such as the total length of the Nile river.

    d. A sports fact. This can include such things as which team won the play-offs or the three latest Triple Crown winners.

    e. Country facts. After choosing a country, students should record such facts as the area, population, capital, two largest cities, and principal products.

A sample worksheet at the end of this unit suggests a format for students to list the facts and page numbers where the facts were located.

5. After using *The Information Please Almanac* students should check for the same information from four other sources:

   a. An older edition of *The Information Please Almanac*. It would be best if the earlier edition were *at least* three years older than the one used to fill in the first column.

   b. Another almanac. This gives students direct experience with similarities and differences among almanacs.

   c. An encyclopedia. This source provides longer entries and is a nice contrast to the almanac.

   d. Some other source. Teachers may wish to let students choose or may assign them to check other sources such as a desk encyclopedia, magazines or newspapers, more general books, the *Guinness Book of World Records*, and so on. As students find information, they should list the facts and page numbers where they found them.

6. Have students look for any differences in the facts they have collected and try to explain why discrepancies occurred. Does the copyright date of the work affect this? Do the two almanacs agree? What does the encyclopedia include that the others do not, and vice versa?

7. Finally, which tool do students like best? Least? Which do they think is most trustworthy? Why? When would they use an almanac? Which one? When would they use an encyclopedia? What did they like or dislike about the other sources?

8. After groups have finished the worksheets and worked through the questions in steps 6 and 7, discuss the results with students. Can the class arrive at some consensus? What guidelines can they formulate on using these sources and the quality of information they contain?

CONSIDERATIONS:
1. For a discussion of the discrepancies and similarities among sources it may be helpful for each group to prepare an overhead transparency patterned after their worksheet.

2. As a follow-up students could pass on their discoveries to students in another class or create materials to display in the school library media center for the various sources.

WORKSHEET FOR COMPARISON SOURCES

Type	*Information Please*	*Information Please*	Other almanac	Encyclopedia	Other source
Title					
Date					
Famous person (Birth/death dates; 2 facts)					
Economic figures					
Geographical fact					
Sports data					
Country facts (Name; area; population; capital; 2 largest cities, principal products)					

Knowlton, Jack. *Geography from A to Z; A Picture Glossary.*
New York: Thomas Y. Crowell, 1988.

SUMMARY: An alphabetical listing of basic geographical terms ranging from archipelago to zone. Uncluttered pictures by Harriett Barton clearly illustrate each term.

GRADE LEVEL: 2nd and 3rd grades

CURRICULUM AREA: Geography; Semantic Mapping; Classification

OBJECTIVE: To reinforce student knowledge of basic geographical terms

ACTIVITY:
Materials: Overhead projector pens, transparencies, overhead projector

1. At the conclusion of a geography unit, have students (either individually or in groups) use the technique of semantic mapping to show their understanding of any geographic terms studied. Students should organize and classify terms in a manner that makes sense to them. An example is given at the end of this unit.

2. When students have finished the map, they can make a transparency of their work. (They can either write directly on the transparency film or make a black and white master copy for machine-made transparencies.) Color pens could be used to emphasize or clarify the groupings.

3. Transparencies can be shown to the entire class for discussion or review purposes. Final products should vary since individual classification schemes may be different. But mapping should be based on the meaning of terms, not external factors such as word length.

CONSIDERATIONS:
1. Forty-nine terms are included in the sample map (see accompanying list). Teachers may wish to specify a minimum or maximum number of terms to be included.

2. The book can be used for student reference. If the teacher wishes, a list of definitions can be given to students first.

SAMPLE GEOGRAPHIC TERMS MAP

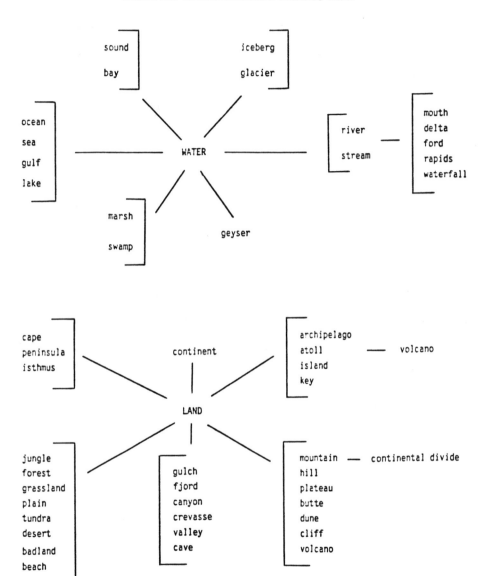

WORDS IN GEOGRAPHIC MAP

archipelago	delta	iceburg	plateau
atoll	desert	island	rapids
badland	dune	isthmus	reef
bay	ford	jungle	river
beach	forest	key	sea
butte	fjord	lake	sound
canyon	geyser	marsh	stream
cape	glacier	mountain	swamp
cave	grassland	mouth	tundra
cliff	gulch	ocean	valley
continent	gulf	peninsula	volcano
continental divide	hill	plain	waterfall
crevasse			

The World Almanac and Book of Facts 1987.
New York: Pharos Books, 1986.

SUMMARY: A compendium of geographical, political, social, historical, and scientific knowledge with an emphasis on listing of facts and figures.

GRADE LEVEL: 5th and 6th grades

CURRICULUM AREA: Library Skills; Question Analysis

OBJECTIVES: To teach students to use an almanac and an index
To give students practice in using an almanac

ACTIVITY:
Materials: Multiple copies of *The World Almanac* (at least two), index cards

1. Explain to students what an almanac is and what types of information it contains.

2. Show students how to use the index. Overhead transparencies of the topics chosen for illustration can help students follow the discussion while they use the almanacs. Students may work in groups of two or three if necessary.

3. Have each student use the almanac to write three quiz questions. The questions should be written so that the index is used to find the answer. Students should write questions of varying difficulty in terms of the way the index is used in finding the answer and then a point system can be used to rate the difficulty of questions. Have students give the index term, answer, page number, suggested point value and justification, and their name on each card in addition to the question itself. For example:

A.   What is the zip code of Bozeman, Montana?

        ANSWER   59715

        PAGE   244

        INDEX TERM   Zip Codes

        POINT VALUE 1, WHY? "Zip code" sends you to
                                      the right table

        NAME   Carol Doll

B.   How many people died in car accidents in 1980?

        ANSWER   52,600

        PAGE   780

        INDEX TERM   Automobiles

        POINT VALUE 2, WHY? "see" reference at "Cars"

        NAME   Carol Doll

C. What star was originally named Virginia McMath?

   ANSWER   Ginger Rogers

   PAGE   391

   INDEX TERM   Actors, Actresses

   POINT VALUE 3, WHY? Neither "star" nor "name" is
                          in the index

   NAME   Carol Doll

The variety of questions can help students recognize the different index skills they use and the need for question analysis when obvious terms do not work.

4. Divide the class into two teams and have an "almanac bee," following the procedure used for spelling bees. The student in the front of each line should have a copy of *The World Almanac*. If one student is unable to answer in the alloted time, the question passes to the other team. The almanac will pass from the student unable to find the answer to the next person in line.

CONSIDERATIONS:

1. All copies of *The World Almanac* should be the same edition, but it is not necessary to have the most recent year.

2. It may be beneficial to wait for several days after students write the questions before playing the game to better reinforce the skills being taught.

3. It is possible to do this activity with only two copies of *The World Almanac*. In this case it may be necessary to give students several days to write their questions so they have enough time to get to the books.

The World Book Encyclopedia.
Chicago: World Book, Inc., 1988.

SUMMARY: This twenty-two volume set attempts to gather introductory information on all topics.

GRADE LEVEL: 3rd through 6th grades

CURRICULUM AREA: Social Studies; Library Skills; Evaluating Information

OBJECTIVES: To increase student knowledge about specific countries
To give students an opportunity to practice encyclopedia skills

ACTIVITY:
Materials: Worksheets

1.   This activity is designed to be part of a larger classroom unit, once the topic has been introduced and students are ready to investigate on their own.

2.   Teach students (or review for them) what an encyclopedia is, how it is organized, and how to use it. The school library media specialist can help with this.

3.   Then assign students or allow them to pick a topic. If countries are being studied, a student may investigate Australia.

4.   Explain to students they will not be copying from the encyclopedia, but using it to find facts they will use later in a written or oral report. Give students a worksheet (see sample at the end of this unit) and discuss it with them.

5.   Let students use the encyclopedias to fill in the first column on the worksheets.

6.   Have students use at least two other sources to look for the same information and fill in the last two columns on the worksheet. At least one of these last two sources should be a second encyclopedia. It may be a totally different encyclopedia or an earlier edition of *The World Book Encyclopedia*.

7.   Have students compare, contrast, and evaluate the sources they used to find information about their topic. They should identify the strengths and weaknesses of each source. Then, looking at the information they located, students should determine which information or type of information is the same, which is different, and try to suggest and support reasons for any discrepancies noted.

8. After this analysis of information gathered, have students prepare their reports.

9. A final class discussion should explore student reactions to and experiences with the information sources. Which do they believe to be the best? The worst? Why? How will their experiences help them in future information searches?

CONSIDERATIONS:

1. This technique can work for any research topic, whether it is social studies, science, or anything else covered in the curriculum.

2. Sometimes it is helpful if students work in pairs with one student reading the encyclopedia and the other filling out the worksheet.

3. This activity encourages students to do their own writing and helps break the habit of copying directly from the encyclopedia.

4. As a supplementary activity, students could cut up their worksheets into nineteen pieces by separating the categories. These pieces could be gathered (in the separate categories) and then randomly redistributed. Students would then create a report about an imaginary country. Results would be evaluated on how "realistically" students were able to integrate their random pieces.

SAMPLE WORKSHEET

Student Names _____

_____

Country   _____

	First encyclopedia	Second source	Third source
Name	_____	_____	_____
Vol.	_____	_____	_____
Date	_____	_____	_____
Country	_____		
Continent	_____		
Area (sq. mi.)	_____		
Capital	_____		
Population	_____		
Language	_____		
Chief products	_____		
Money	_____		
Type of government	_____		
Climate	_____		
History Discovered	_____		
How settled	_____		
Native people	_____		
Animals	_____		

	First encyclopedia	Second source	Third source
Plants			
Rivers			
Recreation			
Industry			
Natural resources			
Famous people			
Country today			
Other			

Fact Books

This chapter deals with those titles that present or summarize facts. The *Guinness Book of World Records* is one example that tends to be very popular with young people.

In these books the emphasis is on the facts or pieces of information. Usually, the author or editor makes little or no effort to explain, present background, or draw conclusions. While this can simplify the book, it can also result in a dry, unimaginative listing of information. This tendency can be overcome in a number of ways, such as the types of unusual information or events listed in *Encyclopedia Brown's Third Fact Book*.

Fact books should be well organized so that the information they contain is more readily available to the reader. Chapters or sections should be arranged in a logical order. A table of contents is often helpful. In larger books, an index can be extremely important. Illustrations or pictures can be included to illuminate information given or to add a humorous touch.

Fact books can and do contain useful information. They serve a function both as a quick source for needed facts and as a place to browse for unusual or interesting information. Some reluctant readers will willingly spend time exploring the entries in *The Guinness Book of World Records*.

Coy, Harold. *The First Book of Presidents.*
New York: Franklin Watts, Inc., 1977.

SUMMARY: Following general information on the office of the president of the United States, brief biographies are given for former presidents.

GRADE LEVEL: 4th and 5th grades

CURRICULUM AREA: U.S. History; Evaluating Information

OBJECTIVE: To increase student knowledge about the presidents of the United States

ACTIVITY:
Materials: Bulletin board, paper, crayons or markers, envelopes

1. Set up the learning center, including Coy's book and the materials listed above. Cover and label the bulletin board.

2. Discuss with students the difference between trivia or fun facts and important information that can broaden understanding of history.

3. Assign each student to a president. Using Coy's book and other sources where necessary, the student is to find one trivial fact and one important decision that applies to that man. For example: his clothing store failed; he chose to drop the atom bomb on Japan. The trivial fact and the decision are to be written on the outside of separate envelopes. Each answer (Harry S. Truman) is to be written on a piece of paper and sealed inside. Also on the inside, the student should indicate whether this is a trivial fact or the more important decision and explain why. The envelope is then posted on the bulletin board with the trivial fact or decision showing.

4. Students are free to use Coy's book or other sources to try to identify the president associated with each trivial fact or decision. Also, students should distinguish between trivial facts and more important information and be able to explain these decisions. Each student should regard his or her set of answers as privileged information and not share them with others.

5. After an appropriate period of time (two to three weeks), give a quiz by reading the trivial facts and decisions from the envelopes. Students should write down their responses and indicate whether they are trivial facts or decisions. After students exchange papers, read the trivial facts and decisions again, then open the envelopes and read the answers. Each student can correct the paper received.

6. Either as papers are being corrected or after the quiz, once again discuss the difference between trivia or fun facts and more important information. The contents of the envelopes should provide ample material for consideration. Have students explain how this activity has helped them to better understand how to distinguish between the two.

CONSIDERATIONS:
1. If this activity is too involved, it can be done without the quiz. Students can create a bulletin board using folded construction paper. The fact can be on top, and the president's name can be revealed by lifting the flap.

2. Instead of assigning students to a president, a list of presidents could be posted in the learning center. Then students could volunteer to do an envelope or folded paper and check off the name of the president they investigated.

German, Joan W. *The Money Book.*
New York: Elsevier/Nelson Books, 1981.

SUMMARY: Briefly explains the values of American coins and the dollar bill. Some sample problem situations are presented.

GRADE LEVELS: Kindergarten through 2nd grade

CURRICULUM AREA: Social Studies; Math; Decision making

OBJECTIVES: To introduce students to the various denominations of American coins
To give students an opportunity to practice using money

ACTIVITY:
Materials: Play money of appropriate denominations, items to sell in the "store"

1. Have the students bring items from home (empty, clean boxes, bottles, jars, cans, or cartons) that can be used to set up a play grocery store.

2. Use German's book to introduce students to or reinforce their knowledge of American coins.

3. Have students set up, stock, and price items for the grocery store.

4. The grocery store can function as a learning center or extra-time activity. Students can take turns being clerk or cashiers and customers. This allows them to practice both paying and collecting money. Both clerk and customer should be involved in totaling the bill and collecting change.

5. After students are comfortable with paying and collecting money, discuss with the class the function of money. People earn or receive money in exchange for goods they have or services they perform. They pay money to get goods or services they want.

6. Explain to students that through their work in the store, as both customers and clerks, they have each earned a certain amount of money. (Play money from the store can be used.) Distribute the money to the students.

7. Then tell students they will be able to use their money to buy certain things. These should be normal classroom privileges such as leading the line to the library, running an errand to the office, or passing out papers. Work with students to rank these according to some criteria, such as importance or time involved, and then attach prices to them so students can spend their money to buy these jobs.

8. Continue the experiment for a week or two, so students get a feel for the process. This is a good time to talk about budgeting, or spending money for several cheaper items versus an expensive one.

9. At the conclusion of this unit, discuss this experience with students. Be sure to cover some realities of budgeting, such as some things may cost more than one can afford, or if one buys too many small things there is not enough money for the big item.

CONSIDERATIONS:
1. In the grocery store, it may be better for younger students to buy only one or two items at a time, while older students may need the practice and reinforcement of multiple purchases.

2. It may be desirable to use this activity to support instruction about nutrition, various food groups, or budgeting, especially for older students.

3. To avoid pandemonium, it may be wise to set up some rules for selling. Blank tokens could be made with space for job and day or time. After all privileges have been listed, each child could have a chance to buy one item or spend a certain amount of money. This could be done once or several times.

4. If time permits, the teacher may wish to work with students to devise ways to earn money or barter and trade goods and services.

Guinness Book of World Records.
Edited by Alan Russell. New York: Sterling Publishing Company, 1987.

SUMMARY: A collection of facts about the longest, shortest, biggest, smallest, most, least, or other extreme records for anything and everything from people to animals to things to sporting events.

GRADE LEVEL: 4th through 6th grades

CURRICULUM AREA: Math; Collecting and Evaluating Information

OBJECTIVES: To give students an opportunity to practice measuring and counting
To give students an opportunity to gather and analyze the value of information

ACTIVITY:
Materials: Index cards, rulers, measuring tape, scales, other measuring devices

1. Set up a learning center in the classroom with a copy of *The Guinness Book of World Records* and index cards.

2. Most students will already be familiar with *The Guinness Book of World Records*. Briefly discuss the content of the book or ask students for their favorite entry.

3. Explain to students they are going to create a "Book of Classroom Records" including things like the longest wall, smallest window, thickest book, student who lives farthest from school, and so on. Show them the learning center and tell them to use their imaginations.

4. Students should fill out one index card for each record. By working in pairs they can verify each others measurements. Each card should have the category of measurement, the winner, the winning result, other items measured, and the names of the investigators. For example:

CATEGORY: Lives closest to school

WINNER: John Smith

RESULT: Lives across street

OTHERS CONSIDERED/MEASURED: All students in class

INVESTIGATORS: Ann Jones, Mary Brown

---

5. As the cards accumulate, students may wish to sort them into related groups in the same manner as the book is divided into chapters.

6. At the close of the unit (in two or three weeks) the cards can be kept in a file, put in a scrapbook, or even entered into a computer to be printed out and distributed to the whole class.

7. Discuss with students the value of the information gathered. Is it just interesting or does it have some importance? If so, what? Why? Also, relate this discussion to the *Guinness Book of World Records*.

CONSIDERATIONS:
1. It might be helpful for students to review and perhaps check the winners already gathered in the learning center. In case of disputes, if the original investigators and the verifiers cannot agree, a third team can be appointed.

2. This could be extended to the whole school instead of being limited to the classroom.

Schwartz, David M. *How Much Is a Million.*
Illustrated by Steven Kellogg. New York: Lothrop, Lee and Shepard Company, 1985.

SUMMARY: Using stars, children, and goldfish, Schwartz conveys the idea of the relative size of large numbers.

GRADE LEVEL: Kindergarten through 3rd grade

CURRICULUM AREA: Math

OBJECTIVE: To help students develop the concepts of million, billion, and trillion

ACTIVITY:
Materials: Tissue paper, glue, construction paper with outline figure

1. Starting small, ask students to show one item (fingers can work well here). Write *1* on the board.

2. Ask students to show ten items. Use both figures and markers. Write *10* on the board.

3. Introduce and explore the idea of *100*. Have each student tear ten pieces of tissue paper into ten pieces. Now each student has 100 pieces of tissue paper. Write *100* on the board. Have the students crumple each piece over a pencil and glue it on the construction paper in the outline (star shapes might work nicely).

4. Introduce and explore the idea of 1,000. Write *1,000* on the board. Have ten students bring their completed tissue-paper stars to the front of the room so students can see 1,000 pieces of tissue paper.

5. Introduce and explore the idea of 10,000. Explain if 100 students made the tissue-paper stars, there would be 10,000 pieces of paper. How many classrooms of children would that take? Write *10,000* on the board.

6. Ask students if they know the words *million*, *billion*, and *trillion*. Ask them to explain what they mean. Write the three numbers on the board.

7. Share Schwartz's book with the class.

8. It may be beneficial to discuss million, billion, and trillion after reading the book.

CONSIDERATIONS:
1. While tearing 10 pieces of paper into 100 pieces may be time consuming and messy, the activity will serve to stress the size of the numbers involved. Also, younger students will benefit from the physical manipulation of objects.

2. Teachers may wish to help students determine the total number of pieces of tissue paper glued to the stars they made and then display those stars in the classroom.

Simon, Seymour. *Body Sense, Body Nonsense.*
Illustrated by Dennis Kendrick. New York: J. B. Lippincott, 1981.

SUMMARY: Simon presents familiar sayings about the body such as "drafts cause colds," and then explains why they are or are not true.

GRADE LEVEL: 4th through 6th grades

CURRICULUM LEVEL: Health; Science

OBJECTIVE: To give students an opportunity to apply health knowledge gained in class
To give students a chance to arrive at and defend their positions

ACTIVITY:
Materials: Tagboard, felt markers

1.   At the end of the health unit, the teacher should select sayings from *Body Sense, Body Nonsense* that students have the background to explore.

2.   These sayings can be transferred to tagboard flash cards, with one saying per card.

3.   Divide students into groups, giving each group an equal number of sayings. Students will then determine whether each quote is sense or nonsense and tell why they reached that decision. Textbooks, materials, and information presented in class or the media center collection can be used for background information.

4.   After students have had enough time to answer the questions, groups can take turns presenting a saying and their support of or disagreement with it to the entire class. Students can show the books or magazines that support their argument. Other students or groups may wish to comment on group reports. If there is conflicting information, a discussion could ensue about the differences and a further search for the right answer could begin. Eventually, the teacher may rule on the correctness of each decision and/or supporting reason, and so keep score.

5.   In cases of conflicting information, discuss why the discrepancy in information may have occurred, which source or sources seem to have the best answer and why, and so forth. This can help students become critical users of information.

CONSIDERATIONS:
1.   It is important to select sayings carefully so students legitimately can be expected to answer them. If selections are too hard, students could be frustrated. If selections are too easy, students may not be challenged enough.

2. It is possible to use this same technique and set up a learning center in the classroom containing the sayings on flash cards and available reference books.

3. Teachers could use selected sayings when introducing the health unit to pique student interest. This could also make them more conscious of these sayings and prepare them for the task of deciding whether or not they are correct.

Sobol, Donald J. *Encyclopedia Brown's 3rd Record Book of Weird and Wonderful Facts.*
Illustrated by Sal Murdocca. New York: William Morrow and Company, 1985.

SUMMARY: Sobol has collected a large number of interesting facts on subjects ranging from sports to animals to unusual finds to medicine.

GRADE LEVEL: 4th through 6th grades

CURRICULUM AREA: Current Events; Reading Skills; Collecting and Evaluating Information

OBJECTIVES: To develop in students the habit of reading the newspaper
To have students learn to use library resources to find or check information

ACTIVITY:
Materials: Daily newspapers

1. Briefly introduce students to Sobol's book. Discuss with the class where he could have found these facts.

2. Tell students the class will build their own collection of weird facts based on items found scattered in the local newspaper.

3. Discuss with the class some general guidelines to be used in identifying items for inclusion. Teachers may wish to exclude items from regular features based on unusual facts, such as "Ripley's Believe It or Not."

4. Require students to indicate where each fact came from by giving the name of the newspaper along with the date and page number.

5. Wherever possible, students should use library books to check the veracity of facts found. They should record whether or not the facts were supported in the library source and record where the information was located.

6. Once enough facts have been collected, have students work in groups to produce a news broadcast. Each group can be assigned an area, such as animals or sports. Then each group should select a number of facts to highlight in their portion of the broadcast. Remind students as they write scripts and designate "actors" that a variety of techniques can be used such as interviews, on-the-spot reporting, or a longer human-interest piece. One group should be in charge of overall production, including organization, filming, and providing an anchor person.

7. Videotape the news broadcast. Share the finished tape with the entire class and perhaps others in the school.

CONSIDERATIONS:

1. This could be an on-going project or limited to a week or month.

2. If there is a school newspaper items could be selected to share with the whole school.

3. Students could be sent to interview people in the community to build a file of facts for the local area.

4. The project could be limited to specific subjects only such as sports, animals, or history. Then students could use the library collection to build their own book of facts.

5. If videotaping equipment is not available, a radio broadcast could be taped.

"How To" Books

This chapter deals with those books designed to show the reader how to perform a specific task or tasks. Cookbooks are one common type of book that fits this category. A title may concentrate primarily on the activity and the steps needed to accomplish that activity, or, in addition to the necessary steps, a significant amount of background information can be given. Either approach can be appropriate, depending on such things as age of the intended audience or topic of the book.

These "how to" or instruction books must be well organized. Often directions are given on how to perform a specific task. In this case, the authors must have broken down the procedure in to sequential steps the reader can follow. And, the order in which the steps are given must be workable. In making bread, for example, usually the dough must rise *before* it is put into the oven. Also, the directions must be clearly or completely written so that the reader can follow them successfully and end up with the desired product, whether it is bread, a photograph, or a paper airplane.

Sometimes readers are directed to use or work with potentially dangerous things while performing the indicated procedures. When following a cookbook recipe, for example, a student may need to use a sharp knife or turn on the stove or oven. Authors should anticipate potential dangers and include appropriate instructions. A young child may be told to work with a parent or other responsible adult. Older students may only need to be reminded of pertinent safety precautions. Of course, activities that pose serious hazards should be entirely omitted.

In general, children enjoy instructional books and often have actively searched for them independently when necessary. These titles give children a chance to be actively involved with the materials, instead of the more usual passive reading role. "How to" books can sometimes work well with reluctant readers if books can be found on topics these students enjoy. Also, instructional titles give students the opportunity to develop and practice the skills needed to follow written directions.

Cohen, Daniel. *How to Test Your ESP.*
New York: E. P. Dutton, 1982.

SUMMARY: Cohen defines and gives examples of various types of ESP, followed by tests the readers can use to measure their own psychic abilities.

GRADE LEVEL: 4th through 6th grades

CURRICULUM AREA: Science; Collecting and Evaluating Information; Scientific Method

OBJECTIVE: To give students experience in gathering and interpreting data

ACTIVITY:
  Materials: Pack of playing cards, card-size pieces of blank paper, six six-sided dice and a throwing cup, record sheets or posters

1. Set up a learning center in the classroom. Include Cohen's book and the materials listed above.

2. Discuss ESP with students. Ask how many of them believe in it. It may be helpful to record how many do or do not believe.

3. Explain to students how the learning center is set up and how Cohen's book has four tests they can perform to test their ESP — the Four Ace Test, the Future Ace Test, Sender and Receiver, and Throwing Dice. Encourage students to use the center and keep careful records of their results (see examples at the end of this unit).

4. Record final test results on the sheets or posters prepared.

5. After a period of time, use the posters of results for class discussion. Work with the students to decide whether or not ESP exists.

CONSIDERATIONS:
1. If it is not possible for students to work together on the sender/receiver test, this activity can be done using only the other three tests.

2. This activity can be used to reinforce the idea of scientific method.

3. The more tests the students are able to run, the better the results will be. Twenty runs of Throwing Dice is much better than only two runs.

4. A bulletin board could be used to post and record the test results so the class can easily follow developing patterns.

Four Ace Test

Expected average = 12

Student	Date	Average Hits

Future Ace Test

Expected Average = 12

Student	Date	Average Hits

Sender/Receiver

Expected Score = 5 hits out of 20

Sender	Receiver	Date	Average Hits per 20

Throwing Dice

Expected Score = 1/6 of dice thrown

Student	Date	No. Dice Thrown	1/6 of dice thrown	No. of hits

Forbes, Robin. *Click: A First Camera Book.*
New York: Macmillan Publishing Company, Inc., 1979.

SUMMARY: Simple directions and tips for beginning photographers are accompanied by black and white photographs that clearly illustrate points made.

GRADE LEVEL: 2nd and 3rd grades

CURRICULUM AREA: Art; Visual Literacy

OBJECTIVES: To give students an opportunity to practice taking pictures
To have students learn and apply some of the elements of good photography

ACTIVITY:

Materials: Cameras (one per student or one per group), black and white film, money or supplies to develop film, three-ring notebooks or photo albums

1. Students will need initial instruction on how to use a camera and take pictures. Talk about what makes good pictures.

2. Tell students they will be working in groups to create "concept" albums. Students may either select or be assigned a concept such as size, shape, or color. They will take pictures that show that concept. Forbes's book can give them tips on taking good pictures.

3. Set up a learning center in the classroom where Forbes's book is available for student reference. Students should have a week or two to look at the book. Tell students where the class will go to take pictures (the school yard, a park, etc.).

4. After students know how many pictures they will take (one-half roll or one roll), they should think about what to photograph. Forbes's book can give them suggestions and ideas.

5. Take the students out to shoot one-half of their allotted pictures. Assign numbers to students and match those to the rolls of film. It may be necessary to group students together. For example, if each student will use a total of one roll, assign two students to one roll here (with each getting one-half roll). In step six, they can be grouped again to use their other half roll.

6. Have the film developed. Return the pictures to students. Groups should meet to collectively examine the results so far and discuss what they like and do not like about their pictures. Help students decide what to change or do differently the next time. For example, they may need to get close-ups or change the angle, or they may think of some new examples for their concept.

7. Take students out a second time to use the rest of their film. Again, assign numbers or develop a system to match students and film.

8. Have the film developed. Now the groups can meet to determine which pictures to use (some from each student), what order to put them in, which to use for the title page, and what the title will be.

9. Finished books can be used in kindergarten or first grade or placed on display in the classroom or school library media center.

CONSIDERATIONS:
1. Every student should take some pictures. This is the reason film should be assigned to individuals instead of the group. Also, each student should have at least two pictures included in the finished book.

2. Polaroid cameras could be used, if they are available and if students and teacher are comfortable with them. This would eliminate time needed for developing the film.

3. The books can make a nice exhibit for parents' night.

4. If a preschool or daycare class is nearby, students might like to share their books with children there.

5. Books by Tana Hoban may provide useful ideas or starting points for students. But, student work may be more original if they do not see Hoban's work first.

Goeller, Lee. *How to Make an Adding Machine that Even Adds Roman Numerals.*
Illustrated by Kiyo Komoda. New York: Harcourt Brace Jovanovich, 1979.

SUMMARY: Using egg cartons and marbles, Goeller details the steps involved in making and using an adding machine.

GRADE LEVEL: 4th through 6th grades

CURRICULUM AREA: Math; Problem Solving

OBJECTIVES: To reinforce student knowledge of addition and subtraction
To provide students with a chance to apply problem solving skills

ACTIVITY:
Materials: A collection of containers (egg cartons, ice cube trays, paper divided into squares), markers (marbles, buttons, paper disks), paper, colored crayons or markers

1. Set up a learning center in the classroom. Include the collection of materials.

2. Briefly review addition and subtraction with students. Remind them about carrying and borrowing.

3. Explain the learning center has been set up and challenge students (either individually or in groups) to invent a machine that anyone can use to add and subtract. Remind them to think carefully about what happens when they add or subtract. Teachers may wish to rule out the mere counting of objects.

4. Students who believe they have succeeded can make appointments to show their results to the teacher.

5. At the end of the unit, schedule show and tell for all inventors to show their results to the class. Goeller's machine should be part of this exhibition.

6. The adding machines can be left on display in the classroom for students to work with.

CONSIDERATIONS:
1. Toward the end of a unit, a student (using Goeller's book) could be assigned the task of building and learning to use the machine described in the book.

2. Students could work on the project in the learning center either individually or in groups.

3. The finished machines could make a nice display for parents' night.

4. Advanced or older students could be challenged to invent a machine that will add and subtract Roman numerals or one which multiplies and divides.

Johnson, Hannah Lyons. *Let's Bake Bread.*
New York: Lothrop, Lee and Shepard Company, 1973.

SUMMARY: Step-by-step instructions for baking bread from the list of supplies needed through clean-up.

GRADE LEVEL: Kindergarten through 6th grade

CURRICULUM AREA: Science; Social Studies; Scientific Method

OBJECTIVES: To give students direct experience with one way bread is made
To introduce students to yeast as a plant and its role in bread making

ACTIVITY:
Materials: Supplies to make bread, access to running water and stove, beakers, measuring spoons, yeast, thermometers, alternatives to sugar and water

1. Introduce the topic of bread to children and discuss it with them.

2. Use Johnson's book to show students the steps to follow in making bread.

3. Mix up a batch of bread. Let all students get involved in some way. Make sure students notice that bread rises and make note of the difference between the size of the first-formed loaf and the final loaf.

4. Bake the bread and eat it.

5. Ask students if they know why the bread dough changed in size. It may be helpful to list the ingredients used on the board. Ask why the yeast makes bread rise (it is a fungus that uses sugar and releases carbon dioxide gas). Then guide students in developing questions based on varying the three key ingredients:

yeast — Do different quantities, ages, or temperatures of yeast change the amount of reaction?

sugar — What if there is no sugar? Can there be too much or too little sugar? What if salt, soda, or cornstarch are used instead?

hot water — Can the water be too hot or too cold? Does it matter how much water is used? Will other liquids work?

Also, what about the location where the bread is put to rise? (Anything from a freezer to refrigerator to a heated oven may be suggested.)

6. Work with students to devise an experiment to test some of the questions raised. It is not necessary to make a loaf of bread each time. The yeast and other ingredients can be mixed in a beaker or cup and the ensuing reaction can be observed. Except where the quantity is the variable, the beaker size and amounts of ingredients should remain constant for control purposes. It is probably best to use Johnson's quantities as the standard.

7. Carefully record the results and discuss them with students. What worked best? What did not work? Why?

CONSIDERATIONS:
1. If bread making is a new activity for the teacher, it may be wise to either try it at home first or enlist an experienced volunteer to help.

2. All students should be able to knead the bread since it is hard to overwork the dough. Be sure their hands are clean.

3. This activity could be good preparation for a field trip to a bakery or classroom visit from a professional baker.

Oechsli, Helen, and Kelly Oechsli. *In My Garden: A Child's Gardening Book.*
New York: Macmillan Publishing Company, 1985.

SUMMARY: An introduction and guide to vegetable gardening for children, from soil preparation through harvesting.

GRADE LEVEL: Kindergarten through 3rd grade

CURRICULUM AREA: Science; Scientific Method

OBJECTIVES: To teach students about seeds and plant growth
To give students experience in planting, tending, and harvesting plants

ACTIVITY:
Materials: Seeds or small plants, containers for plants (e.g., milk cartons), trays for draining water, fertilizer

1. Discuss vegetables and their life cycle with the students. Tell students they will be growing vegetables in the classroom.

2. Using the Oechslis' book as a guide, explain the steps that will be followed. It may be helpful to list the steps on the board or on a piece of butcher paper or poster board.

3. The Oechslis' list some vegetables that can be grown inside in pots and give directions for planting and caring for them. Discuss these directions with students. Guide the students in exploring and questioning the instructions. Have the students suggest ways to test the directions.

4. Have seeds or small plants available and plant them. As the plants grow, the students should be involved in tending them, from thinning to weeding to harvest. Also, implement some of their suggestions for testing the instructions. Some plants may get too little or too much water; some may not be thinned; some may or may not be fertilized; some may or may not be turned to get sun on all sides; and so on. Carefully record the various treatments and the results.

5. As the vegetables ripen, students should share in harvesting and eating them. It may be possible to make a salad from the produce for the whole class.

6. Some plants may not grow or develop vegetables. Discuss this with students. Compare the various treatments with the end results. Help students understand why some plants grew well and other did not.

CONSIDERATIONS:
1. If possible, ask students to bring milk cartons and other suitable containers from home.

2. Each student should have at least one plant of his or her own that is expected to survive and produce vegetables.

3. If a poster is made of steps to be followed in raising plants, each step can be checked off as it is accomplished. For example:

   - Prepare soil and container
   - Plant seeds
   - Water the plants
   - Thin the plants

4. Some school grounds might offer a place for a small garden, possibly right outside the classroom.

Russell, Helen Ross. *Small Worlds: A Field Trip Guide.*
Boston: Little, Brown and Company, 1972.

SUMMARY: Russell discusses the small insects one can find in microhabitats.

GRADE LEVEL: Kindergarten through 3rd grade

CURRICULUM AREA: Science; Applying Information; Language Arts

OBJECTIVES: To make students aware of the small habitats that surround us
To give students an opportunity to observe microhabitats

ACTIVITY:
Materials: Tape recorder, tape

1. Talk to students about microhabitats. Pay particular attention to those portions most appropriate to the area(s) to be explored. It may be helpful to have some specimens to share with students.

2. Tell students they will be making a "guided tour" on tape of microhabitats on the school grounds. The first step will be a silent walking tour. The students' assignment is to look quietly for some of the things mentioned in Russell's book while the teacher leads the walk.

3. Then each student may be assigned to or asked to find the tour stop he or she will present on the tape. At the stop, the student should locate an element of a microhabitat, identify it, decide how to describe it and what to say about it (with the help of the teacher, Russell's book, and library research), and tell how to get to the next tour stop.

4. When everyone is ready, have a dress rehearsal.

5. Record the tape, with each student speaking his or her own lines into the tape recorder in order from first to last tour stop. The tape may be made either inside or at the tour stops.

6. The entire class should take the guided tour before making the tape available to other classes.

CONSIDERATIONS:
1. It may be possible to study a microhabitat (close to or within the classroom) for a more extended period of time. This could give students a chance to see "daily life" and changes which occur.

2. The school library media center could be helpful when trying to identify specimens not found in Russell's book.

3. If a video camera is available, this could be a videotaped "Television Nature Special." However, tape recorders and players tend to be more portable than video equipment.

Simon, Seymour. *The Paper Airplane Book.*
New York: The Viking Press, 1971.

SUMMARY: An exploration of the physical principles that make paper airplanes fly, with directions for making or adapting several different ones.

GRADE LEVEL: 5th and 6th grades

CURRICULUM AREA: Science; Applying Information

OBJECTIVES: To introduce students to the physics of plane flight
To give students an opportunity to apply some of the principles presented

ACTIVITY:
Materials: Paper, cellophane tape, thread, two ping pong balls, paper clips, scissors

1. Introduce students to topic of paper airplanes, and discuss student experiences with them.

2. Use Simon's book to present information to students about lift and thrust. Pages 8 through 17 are especially effective and have several demonstrations that are helpful to perform.

3. With students, fold the paper airplanes on pages 18 and 19. Fly them in the gym or on the playground. It may be appropriate to show students how to use paper clips to adjust flight.

4. Announce to students there will be a paper airplane contest. Leave Simon's book in the classroom and encourage students to consult the book for guidance in building their paper airplanes.

5. After a period of time (two to three weeks), use the gym or playground for contest flights. It might be best to have several categories, such as: longest flight, best landing, hardest landing by a plane that is still flyable, best loop, and closest to target.

6. Review the principles of flight with students. Discuss what students learned as they applied those principles to their own planes: What worked, what did not work, and why? Why did specific planes win in a particular category? Were there any trade offs to make, such as more control for less distance?

CONSIDERATIONS:
1. It would be best to post the categories before the contest. Then students could use the physical principles learned to create planes to perform in specific ways.

2. It would be best to decide in advance on limits or number of planes per student or per category, and whether or not the same plane can be entered in more than one category.

Self-Help Books

A self-help book is one designed to give guidance, advice, or assistance to children. Topics can vary from how to write to dealing with feelings to staying safe on the street, in the park, or at the shopping center. Regardless of the specific topic, the purpose of these self-help titles is to suggest behaviors, actions, or activities for children in specific situations.

Above all, the information in these titles should be accurate and appropriate. If the child is supposed to follow the book's suggestions, then the activities or behaviors should be suitable and conform with today's society. Any recommended activities should match the developmental or chronological age of the intended audience; and the child should be able to successfully and safely follow the instructions.

Some care should be taken in the use of these self-help titles. Many of these books are on innocuous subjects, such as how to write or what to see in New York City. Other titles, however, deal with more sensitive topics, such as how to adjust to divorce or a death in the family. Many of the books on these personal topics are well written and an important part of this genre. However, teachers or media specialists without psychological training are advised to be cautious when using them with children.

A well-written, accurate self-help book can be very useful in a classroom situation. Some of these books can be used by children independently, which can then free the teacher to do other things. Some work well in learning centers. Some students prefer to use books to explore certain topics and some self-help books work well for these students. Overall, self-help books are a genre that can be quite valuable to both students and teachers.

Aliki. *Feelings.*
New York: Greenwillow Books, 1984.

SUMMARY: Using a variety of situations, Aliki presents various feelings common to children such as jealousy, anger, hurt, happiness, or pride.

GRADE LEVEL: Kindergarten through 2nd grade

CURRICULUM AREA: Health; Critical Thinking

OBJECTIVES: To increase students' awareness of their own feelings
To give students a nonthreatening situation in which to discuss feelings

ACTIVITY:
Materials: Drawing paper or transparencies, appropriate pens

1.   Read Aliki's book.

2.   Discuss feelings with the class, and help students generate a list of feelings.

3.   Have students work in pairs, and assign one of the feelings from the list to each pair. Students should work together to: draw a picture of their feeling; give an example of when they feel that way; pretend they feel that way and show how they would look, stand, what they would say or do, and so on.

4.   After students have worked on their assigned feelings, all pairs should share their results with the class. They can act out their feelings. Pictures can be posted or transparencies projected.

5.   Share some portions of Aliki's book with the class. Did they think of some things Aliki did not, and vice versa? Do they agree with Aliki? What things does Aliki say that they like? What things do they like that the class did? Why?

CONSIDERATIONS:
1.   An opaque projector could be used to share Aliki's pictures with the class.

2.   It may be helpful to leave Aliki's book in the classroom for students to examine after the session is over.

3.   The teacher may wish to extend this activity over several days.

4.   In some cases this would work better as a whole-class activity than as a group activity.

Benjamin, Carol Lea. *Writing for Kids.*
New York: Thomas Y. Crowell, 1985.

SUMMARY: An introduction to writing for children, from how to get started to the mechanics of writing to editing.

GRADE LEVEL: 4th through 6th grades

CURRICULUM AREA: Creative Writing; Evaluating Information

OBJECTIVES: To give students experience in writing
To introduce students to keeping a journal

ACTIVITY:

Materials: Notebooks, poster board or transparencies, appropriate pens

1. Introduce the unit to students. Tell them they will all keep a daily journal for the next month (or other period of time).

2. Use the first chapter of Benjamin's book for the "fill-in-the-blank" exercise to start students thinking and writing. The comments could be dictated to students, overhead transparencies could be used, or the exercise could be written on the blackboard. This experience should be the students' first journal entry.

3. Inform students they are to make daily journal entries, and that they will turn in these journals on a weekly basis.

4. It may be appropriate to leave Benjamin's book in the classroom. If a student did an exercise from the book, that could count for one day's journal entry.

5. After the students have kept daily journals for the allotted period of time, assign them to groups. Each group is to formulate a list of five to ten tips they would offer to others on writing daily journal entries. The lists could be general or on a more limited topic such as "getting started" or "what to do when you have nothing to say."

6. Each group should make a poster or overhead transparency to share their tips with the whole class. Have each group present and discuss their work.

7. As a concluding activity, return to Benjamin's book. Have the students evaluate the book's content. What portions were most helpful? Least helpful? Would they add anything to it? Do they believe Benjamin's advice is wrong in any way?

CONSIDERATIONS:

1. It may not be necessary to grade student notebooks. Work on grammar, sentence structure, and punctuation can come through other exercises. In this case, student notebooks are turned in only to ensure students are truly writing in them.

2. It may even be beneficial to assure students that their work will not be read, only checked off. This may make it easier for some students to make journal entries.

Leranges, Peter. *A Kid's Guide to New York City.*
New York: Gulliver Books, Harcourt Brace Jovanovich Publishers, 1988.

SUMMARY:　After presenting information about contemporary New York City and its history, this book suggests sightseeing activities for children. Games and other activities are also included.

GRADE LEVEL:　3rd through 6th grades

CURRICULUM AREA:　Language Arts; Collecting and Applying Information

OBJECTIVES:　To increase students' knowledge of their school
To provide students with an opportunity to practice communicating information through writing
To give students a practical research experience

ACTIVITY:
Materials: Three-ring notebook, paper, dividers, a "sister" classroom in another school for exchange of final products

1. Briefly share the Leranges book with students. Summarize the types of information and activities found in the book.

2. Tell students they will write a guide to their class or school to exchange with another group. Work with the class to compile a list of appropriate subject headings, such as:

   - meet the teachers

   - this is the principal

   - exploring the playground

   - what to expect in the cafeteria (maybe explore the options between hot and cold lunch)

   - history of the school

   - biography of the person the school is named for

   - what can be found in the media center

   - rules and regulations

   - what every student should know

3. Students, either in teams or individually, should be assigned topics and gather information on their school or class to show the exchange class the interesting and exciting things about their own situation.

4. Then the research results should be written up and a clean copy presented for inclusion in the notebook. The dividers can label different sections.

5. It may be appropriate to illustrate some sections with drawings, maps, charts, or Polaroid pictures.

6. The final tour books should be exchanged and displayed in the classrooms for students to look at in their spare time.

CONSIDERATIONS:

1. This may be either a general guide or one appropriate for a specific grade level or for new students.

2. In gathering information for this project, students may wish to conduct interviews and begin to build an oral history collection of audiotapes.

3. This activity could be done at the beginning of the year to help students become acquainted with their school or grade. Or, it could be done at the end of the year to record and pass on students' accumulated knowledge.

4. Students may wish to create a videotaped tour to introduce themselves to their exchange school.

5. If it is not possible to do this activity in conjunction with another school, it could also work to exchange tour books with another classroom in the same school.

6. If compatible hardware and software are available, the tour book could be on a microcomputer disk. Then disks could be exchanged.

Marsano, William. *The Street Smart Book: How Kids Can Have Fun and Stay Safe.*
New York: Julian Messner, 1985.

SUMMARY: Presents strategies to avoid or deal with potentially dangerous situations where children are approached by strangers. Includes brief fictional segments to support safety tips.

GRADE LEVEL: Kindergarten through 6th grade

CURRICULUM AREA: Personal Safety; Language Arts; Applying Information

OBJECTIVES: To give students information about or remind them of potentially dangerous situations

To suggest strategies to students for avoiding or escaping from dangerous situations

To provide older students an opportunity to create a learning experience for younger students

ACTIVITY:
1. Briefly introduce Marsano's book to older students (fourth, fifth, or sixth grades). Discuss some strategies for children to stay safe.

2. Divide the class into groups. Each group will gather safety information from Marsano's book or from additional research in the school library media center. The teacher may wish to assign topics to prevent duplication of effort.

3. Using the information, each group will integrate the main points into a skit. The skit should present a possible situation and demonstrate appropriate strategies for a child to follow to safely get help. Marsano's book gives four examples in the fifth chapter. Have students practice performing the skit.

4. Older students will visit a classroom of younger students and perform their skit. It probably would be appropriate to summarize tips before and after their skit.

CONSIDERATIONS:
1. This activity is designed for more than one class of students so teachers may need to do some initial planning and coordination.

2. It may be appropriate for teachers to assign situations to students (e.g., a man approaches you in the park; a woman says your mother sent her), and then have students fill in the details.

3. It might be beneficial to have groups perform the skits in their own classroom before going to see the younger students.

4. In some situations, a contest format could be used. Then the best skits could be taken to another classroom or used as part of an all-school safety assembly.

Ward, Hiley H. *Feeling Good about Myself.*
Philadelphia: Westminster Press, 1983.

SUMMARY: In chapters that deal with subjects such as boredom, jealousy, swearing, and neighbors, Ward briefly presents a situation, asks thought-provoking questions, and suggests several strategies for dealing with the problem.

GRADE LEVEL: 5th and 6th grades

CURRICULUM AREA: Language Arts; Critical Thinking

OBJECTIVES: To have students think critically about advice columns in newspapers

To have students logically work toward and evaluate a response to questions in advice columns

ACTIVITY:

Materials: Advice columns from newspapers, such as "Ann Landers," "Dear Abby," "Ask Beth," etc.

1. Collect several advice columns from newspapers with issues pertinent to students. Separate the reader's letter to the column from the writer's official response, labeling them so they can be paired again later.

2. Discuss advice columns with students. Do they read them? Which one(s)? Why or why not? Do they agree with the advice given? Tell students they will have a chance to try writing advice.

3. Present the situation(s) to students. The class can be divided into groups or this can be a learning center activity. Explain to students they are to write a response to the situation as if they were the advice columnist. Ward's book can be used as a reference and may help students clarify their thinking.

4. After the students have finished their responses, the published answers can be shared. Students can decide which response they prefer and should support their position.

CONSIDERATIONS:
1. Students may all work on the same situations or the class may be divided and each group of students may work on their own set of client letters. In this case, groups could share with the entire class the original letter, their response, and the published response. Then the class could discuss the situation and decide which solution they prefer.

2. It would also be possible to use this technique as an extra-curricular activity, and the published letters and client responses could be gathered in a notebook.

Wilt, Joy. *A Kid's TV Guide: A Children's Book about Watching TV Intelligently.*
Chicago: Children's Press, 1982.

SUMMARY: Wilt explores the pros and cons of watching television, and gives tips for more critical viewing.

GRADE LEVEL: 3rd and 4th grades

CURRICULUM AREA: Social Studies; Critical Thinking

OBJECTIVE: To make students more critical viewers of television commercials

ACTIVITY:
1. Talk to students about the function of television commercials, explaining how advertisers pay for the programs we see free while trying to sell us a product. Wilt does a good job of discussing this.

2. Talk about some of the negative aspects of television commercials, such as how some products look better on television than in real life, how some things are not good for you, or how some commercials try to make you believe things that are not true.

3. Assign students to carefully watch and record a commercial during a specific program, perhaps on Saturday morning. Each student should pick one commercial and come to class with a list of its claims and problems or fallacies in it. Ask students if they have had any bad personal experiences with television commercials.

4. Discuss with students ways to think more critically about television commercials. Wilt has a list of questions on pages 122 and 123.

5. Work with students to identify one or two products to investigate. First, identify claims made by the advertisers and the impressions the ads communicate. Then have students, either as a whole class or in groups, critically examine the product. Which advertising claims were correct? Which were false? What looked better in the ad than in real life? What did the ad leave out or forget to mention?

6. Finally, have students write a commercial they believe more accurately presents the product.

7. Discuss this activity and ask students how it may have changed their future reactions to television commercials.

CONSIDERATIONS:
1. It may promote discussion if a videotape of certain commercials was available. Then everyone could see and discuss the same things.

2. The teacher may wish to ask students if they know of any good television commercials, for example those on fire safety, and discuss those with them.

3. This activity would also work with radio, newspaper, or magazine advertising.

4. If a video camera is available, the teacher may wish to have students make a videotape of their rewritten commercial.

Contemporary Issue Books

This category includes those titles that either through content or the way information is presented deal with or allow the teacher to explore topics of current concern or interest, such as energy, solid waste, or the Loch Ness monster. These are topics without a definite answer or solution. Often different people or groups of people have different opinions about the best or the correct answer or response to a situation. Did the National Park Service respond correctly to forest fires in Yellowstone National Park in the summer of 1988? Is there a Loch Ness monster? How should society deal with solid waste disposal?

Various opinions or sides to these contemporary issues come up. Therefore, the potential exists for students to explore the issues, to investigate the pros and cons of various points of view, to discuss the arguments, and to form and support their own opinions. This could be a good way to encourage critical thinking. Students can be guided to realize a book may present only part of an issue and that different books may present different opinions or even contradict each other. Students can learn the benefits of gathering information from more than one source to help them decide on and defend their own opinions.

These contemporary issues titles may be biased or dated. With proper guidance, these titles can present a valid opportunity for students to question the accuracy or point of view of the material presented. This is also an excellent opportunity for students to apply library skills and to use the school library media center as they work to update information. Overall, books on contemporary issues are needed in the school curriculum.

Ingraham, Claire R., and Leonard W. Ingraham. *An Album of Women in American History.*
New York: Franklin Watts, Inc., 1972.

SUMMARY: Briefly discusses prominent women and contributions of women throughout American history in the struggle for equality and women's rights.

GRADE LEVEL: 5th and 6th grades

CURRICULUM AREA: U.S. History; Collecting and Evaluating Information

OBJECTIVES: To make students aware of the role of women in the history of the United States
To make students aware of female stereotypes
To give students experience in gathering and interpreting information

ACTIVITY:
1.   Divide students into groups. Each group will research the role of women in some segment of American history. The Ingrahams' book can suggest topics and serve as a starting point for research.

2.   Each group will briefly report its findings to the class. It may be appropriate to limit the presentation times.

3.   Discuss with students the status of women in American society today. Elicit student reactions and beliefs.

4.   Mention that sometimes subtle forms of stereotyping may occur that reflect the way women are perceived. One place this can happen is in children's books.

5.   Using the same groups as before, have students look at children's picture books to see how women are portrayed in both words and pictures. Assign each group a decade: the 1980s, the 1970s, the 1960s, etc. Each group should look at a specified number of books (five to ten) that were published during the assigned decade and prepare and give an oral report. Students should summarize briefly the position or role of women in society in their decade and relate that to the picture books they examine. For example, do books from the 1960s reflect the changing status of women? Is there a time lag? Has there been any change in the way women are portrayed?

6.   After the reports are presented, discuss the overall results with the class. See if students come to any conclusions or notice any trends.

CONSIDERATIONS:
1. It would be possible to do this activity without the initial student reports. The teacher could give any needed background information (using the Ingrahams' book) and then start with step 3.

2. When students give the oral reports, it may be helpful to summarize briefly their findings on the blackboard to facilitate later discussion.

3. Students may wish to share portions of the picture books (text or illustrations) while giving their reports. Many picture books can be shared with larger groups.

Pringle, Laurence. *Throwing Things Away: From Middens to Resource Recovery.*
New York: Thomas Y. Crowell, 1986.

SUMMARY: An exploration of garbage, from historical times to contemporary landfills, recycling, and environmental concerns.

GRADE LEVEL: 5th and 6th grades

CURRICULUM AREA: Social Studies; the Environment; Evaluating Information

OBJECTIVES: To make students aware of the problems and concerns of waste disposal, including its environmental impact and recycling
To help students realize that not all information in a book is current

ACTIVITY:
1. This activity is designed to be used following initial classroom instruction on refuse and refuse disposal. Pringle's book can be used as a source of information and its bibliography can lead to additional books and articles.

2. Divide students into groups. Each group will seek current information about garbage, landfills, environmental impact of waste, or recycling. Possible information sources are listed below. It is suggested that each group be assigned one or more information source for one or more of the suggested topics: magazines, newspapers (local and state), television (local and national news), radio, and books (with older and newer titles).

3. It may be desirable to have some groups do an opinion survey of some people in the community. This can provide information about local concerns to compare with information from national or state level sources. Once questions are formed, the following people could be interviewed by phone or in person: local officials, companies involved in waste management or recycling, neighbors or local residents, and fellow students.

4. Have groups prepare a brief report of their findings to present to the class. They should be sure to show differences or similarities between their findings and Pringle's work.

5. The point that not all information can be found in books and that not all printed information is in agreement or guaranteed to be correct should be emphasized. Also, have students identify the strengths and weaknesses of the source(s) they used.

CONSIDERATIONS:
1. This same technique could be used with other current topics such as acid rain or drug abuse.

2. It would be possible to set this up as a learning-center activity instead of a whole-class project.

Rabinowich, Ellen. *The Loch Ness Monster.*
New York: Franklin Watts, Inc., 1979.

SUMMARY: A general introduction to the Loch Ness monster, with a discussion of proposed explanations and what evidence is still needed to prove Nessie's existence.

GRADE LEVEL: 3rd and 4th grades

CURRICULUM AREA: Science; Scientific Method; Critical Thinking

OBJECTIVES: To make students aware of the facts and lack of facts about the Loch Ness Monster
To stimulate students to think critically about the issue
To expose students to the role of "hard evidence" in scientific method

ACTIVITY:
1. Discuss the Loch Ness monster with students. Ask what they know or have heard about Nessie. Ask students whether or not they believe in Nessie and why or why not. Why do they think some people believe in Nessie? Why is it some people do not believe in Nessie?

2. Share the information from Rabinowich's book with students. You may wish to read portions of the book.

3. Discuss with students the fact there is no "hard evidence" to prove that Nessie does or does not exist. Scientists looking for Nessie need either physical evidence (body or bones) or a good clear photograph. Even testimony of a trained reliable witness would help. Explore implications of this with students.

4. Discuss Nessie with students again. Ask how many do or do not believe in Nessie, why they do or do not believe, whether or not they have changed their opinion about Nessie during this activity, and why or why not.

5. Discuss with students other topics where people may have different opinions. This can be an "unanswerable" issue, such as whether or not there are UFOs, or a more researchable topic such as whether or not walking under a ladder causes bad luck.

6. Select one or more of the topics for further investigation. What sort of information or evidence would the students need to "answer" the issue. For example, scientists would use a body or bones of the Loch Ness monster to prove it exists. This could be a whole-class project or students could work in groups on various topics.

7. Work with students to design a method to gather information to help "answer" the topic. This could involve an experiment such as walking under ladders to see what happens, or it could involve library research such as finding everything available on UFOs. Then have students use their method to gather information.

8. Finally, discuss with students how well their method(s) worked, what they found out, and what their final answer is.

CONSIDERATIONS:
1. The National Geographic filmstrip set, *Mysteries Old and New* (Washington, D.C.: National Geographic Society, 1982), has a segment on the Loch Ness monster that would work well with this activity.

2. To wrap up, various groups could report to the class using posters, transparencies, charts, and other visual aids.

Radlauer, Ruth. *Yellowstone National Park.*
Chicago: Children's Press, 1985.

SUMMARY: A brief description of the many natural wonders and animals in Yellowstone National Park, accompanied by tips on how to enjoy them safely.

GRADE LEVEL: 4th and 5th grades

CURRICULUM AREA: Current Events; Collecting and Applying Information

OBJECTIVE: To make students aware of differing points of view on the issue of the fires in Yellowstone
To give students an opportunity to prepare for and participate in a debate

ACTIVITY:

Materials: Large map of Yellowstone National Park

1. Introduce students to Yellowstone National Park. Post the map and point out the locations of things discussed. Radlauer's book can provide some basic information.

2. Remind students that there were large forest fires in the park in the summer of 1988. A second map can be colored to show graphically the large amount of land involved in fires. On page 28, Radlauer briefly states park policy on letting fires burn. Not everybody agreed with this policy.

3. Divide students into two groups, one supporting the National Park Service policy and one group opposing it. Students will use the school library media center to research the Yellowstone fires and find evidence to support the point of view their group has been assigned to defend. The information gathered should also include a description of the fires and aftermath.

4. When students have finished their research there will be a classroom debate. Each group will elect a speaker or speakers who will have a chance to give general comments and a position statement. Then each group will have one opportunity to respond to the other's statements. It may be helpful to set a time limit on the speakers.

5. Discuss the debate and information presented. Stress that there are two sides to the issue. It may be useful to vote to see if the class as a whole supports one side or the other.

6. This activity also shows one way in which books or other materials become dated. It may be helpful to have students analyze the information sources they have used. Which ones were published at the time of or shortly after the fires? Which ones were published later? Is there any difference in the tone or quality of information in these sources?

CONSIDERATIONS:

1. It may be possible to use a film, filmstrip, or slides to introduce students to Yellowstone.

2. It may be helpful to divide the class into four groups, two for each position, and have two debates.

3. If a debate is not feasible, each group could make one or two posters presenting and defending their side of the issue.

Shuttlesworth, Dorothy E., and Lee Ann Williams. *Disappearing Energy: Can We End the Crisis?*
New York: Doubleday and Company, 1974.

SUMMARY: Explores the current and potential shortages of electricity, water power, coal, gas, petroleum, trees, and land. Includes predictions of what may happen in the future.

GRADE LEVEL: 5th and 6th grades

CURRICULUM AREA: Social Studies; Current Events; Applying Information

OBJECTIVES: To make students aware of some of the current energy problems
To make students aware of the fact that some books become dated and more current information may be needed
To have students think about the current energy situation and its possible consequences or solution

ACTIVITY:
Materials: Current books, magazines, newspapers, and/or radio and television shows, poster board, paint, markers, or crayons

1. Shuttlesworth and Williams cover a variety of topics. It may be appropriate to investigate all of them, or select those topics of local concern.

2. Discuss with students in general terms the energy crisis, as portrayed by Shuttlesworth and Williams, to introduce the unit.

3. Divide the students into groups. If all groups are to work on the same topic or two topics, share the comments from *Disappearing Energy* with the entire class. If multiple topics will be explored, it may be better to set up a learning center.

4. Students should briefly summarize the most pertinent information from *Disappearing Energy* under three categories: What happened in the past? What is happening in the present? What may happen in the future?

5. Stress to students that the book is over fifteen years old. Resources from the media center and mass media should be used to check the current status of the energy crisis. Students should briefly summarize the results of their search: What is happening in the present? Were Shuttlesworth and Williams correct in their predictions? Why do you think they were right or wrong? What may happen in the future? What solutions are currently proposed? Will these solutions work? Why?

6. Each group is to select information and make a poster. The poster should give the current situation and in some way consider the future, whether it is to predict future events or propose/support possible solutions.

7. Discuss the results of their research with students. Also talk about changes that have occurred since Shuttlesworth and Williams wrote their book. Explore with the class the idea of books becoming dated, possible ways to identify older books, and things the student can do to check or update information in older titles. This can be based on the students' recent experiences.

CONSIDERATIONS:

1. It may be more beneficial to do a series of posters on one topic, such as strip mining. Each group could be responsible for one aspect of the strip mining story, such as current problems, local concerns, solutions that probably will not work, solutions that have potential, the most recent developments, and so on.

2. It may be appropriate to have people concerned with the issue visit the class.

Biographies

Books that intend to portray factually all or part of a person's life are classified here as biographies. The accounts should be real, not fictionalized. The subject of the book can be still living or dead, but in either case the information in the biography must be authentic and accurate.

A good biography presents the subject's life, or a portion of it, in a way that is true to that person's experiences and personality. While triumphs, successes, and accomplishments should be a part of the account, it is important to also include weaknesses, doubts, and failures. These negative aspects are necessary if the whole, human person is to be presented in the biography. Furthermore, omitting the struggles, doubts, and failures can detract from the person's accomplishments by making success seem too easy.

Biographies must be accurate. This is, the information in them should be correct. Mistakes in dates, names, or other areas is inexcusable. Another problem with accuracy arises when certain incidents are omitted because they are deemed unsuitable for children, or because the book is too short and therefore cannot include everything. This can mislead the reader or create false impressions. The author must use extreme care in selecting what to include and what to omit to avoid misleading the reader. Also, the biography's accuracy can be negatively affected by unsubstantiated dialogue in the book. Some experts maintain dialogue should never be used if there is no record that a person actually said the words. Others believe dialogue is acceptable if it can be supported by documentary evidence such as a letter written by the person that the writer has changed to a conversation. In any case, invented or imaginary dialogue should not be included in children's biographies.

Any author approaches his or her work with a certain bias. Some biographies have an almost reverential glow. The task that biographers face is to present a readable account of a real person, complete with strengths and weaknesses, through which children can become acquainted with both famous and lesser known people. Good biographies can help students better understand history, the world around them, other people, and themselves.

Faber, Doris. *Margaret Thatcher: Britain's "Iron Lady."*
New York: Viking Kestrel, 1985.

SUMMARY: Brief biography of Margaret Thatcher from childhood through her work as prime minister. Emphasis is on her intellect and ambition.

GRADE LEVEL: 5th and 6th grades

CURRICULUM AREA: Current Events; Library Skills; Evaluating Information

OBJECTIVES: To increase student awareness of politics in countries other than the United States
To show students that books can become dated and how information from other sources may supplement their content

ACTIVITY:
Materials: Pictures of Thatcher, worksheets

1.   Set up a learning center in the classroom or school library with Faber's biography, worksheets, and pictures of Thatcher.

2.   Introduce the center to students. Explain briefly who Thatcher is, and that this book was written in 1985. Since she is still alive, some events have occurred involving Thatcher since the book was written. Ask students where they might find additional information. They may suggest sources such as other books, magazines, newspapers, or radio and television broadcasts.

3.   Have students read Faber's book.

4.   Have students fill out a worksheet (example included on the next page) to show what can be found about Thatcher in supplemental sources. Stress they should look in sources dated 1985 or later. (Teachers may broaden the scope of this project by having students use materials dated before 1985, and evaluating the content of Faber's book.)

5.   Students should report briefly to the teacher or class on what they found. They should also evaluate the type and tone of the information. Was it factual? Gossipy? Did the source like or respect Thatcher? How do you know? How does information in *Good Housekeeping* differ from information in *Newsweek*? How does the local or nightly news differ from *60 Minutes*? Which source lets you see or get to know Thatcher as a person? Compared to these sources, what are the strengths/ weaknesses of Faber's biography?

BIOGRAPHY WORKSHEET

Person's Name _____

Magazine Articles

Magazine Name   Date   Major Facts

_____   _____   _____

_____

_____

_____   _____   _____

_____

_____

Newspaper Name   Date   Major Facts

_____   _____   _____

_____

_____

Encyclopedia   Volume   Date   Major Facts

_____   _____   ____   _____

_____

_____

TV News   Station   Date   Major Facts

_____   _____   ____   _____

_____

_____

Radio News   Station   Date   Major Facts

_____   _____   ____   _____

_____

_____

CONSIDERATIONS:
1. If this is to be a whole-class project, teachers may wish to include biographies of other public figures, for example, Ronald Reagan, Diana Ross, Dolly Parton, or Joe Montana. Any public figure who is still living, especially if he or she is still active in his or her career, would be appropriate.

2. Also, it would be possible to have the students work in groups. One way to divide the search would be by year. Since Faber's book was published in 1985, one group could be assigned to each year from 1985 to the present year. The search could also be divided by type of source used, for example, magazine or newspaper.

Freedman, Russell. *Lincoln: A Photobiography.*
New York: Clarion Books, 1987.

SUMMARY: A personalized biography of Abraham Lincoln emphasizing the Civil War years, lavishly illustrated with contemporary photographs.

GRADE LEVEL: 5th and 6th grades

CURRICULUM AREA: U.S. History; Creative Writing; Applying Information

OBJECTIVE: To introduce students to Abraham Lincoln
To give students an opportunity for creative writing

ACTIVITY:
1. As part of a unit on the Civil War, make sure at least one copy of Freedman's book is available in the classroom.

2. Students are to read all or part of the book.

3. Based on information in Freedman's book (and optional library research), have the students write an obituary for Lincoln. The emphasis of the writing should be on Lincoln as a person and not just a listing of facts. (How did Lincoln feel about himself? His accomplishments? What did he consider to be the most important of his accomplishments? Did this differ from what the public or history said about him?)

4. If different students read different chapters, the obituaries may differ. It could be quite effective to make a bulletin board of the various obituaries to help create a broader picture of Lincoln.

CONSIDERATIONS:
1. This activity could work equally well for other subjects *if* well-written biographies are available that do more than recite dry facts.

2. All students could participate or this could be an optional learning-center activity.

3. It would be possible for students to make a tape recording of on-the-spot interviews with people sharing their memories of Lincoln instead of writing obituaries.

Fritz, Jean. *Why Don't You Get a Horse, Sam Adams?*
New York: Coward, McCann and Geoghegan, Inc., 1974.

SUMMARY: Fritz details Sam Adams's activities prior to and during early years of the American Revolution.

GRADE LEVEL: 1st and 2nd grades

CURRICULUM AREA: U.S. History; Creative Writing

OBJECTIVES: To introduce students to Sam Adams as an important figure in American Revolution
To give students an opportunity for creative writing

ACTIVITY:
Materials: Writing paper, pencils
1. Read the book to the class.

2. Ask students to close their eyes and pretend that Sam Adams is one of their best friends. Tell them to pick three things they want to say about him, but not to say them out loud.

3. Now, have students write a paragraph about "My Best Friend, Sam Adams." They should have an introductory sentence, the three things in the middle, and a closing sentence.

4. Have students volunteer to read their paragraphs. Post results.

CONSIDERATIONS:
1. Teachers may wish to make an audiotape with introductions instead of having students write paragraphs.

2. This activity will also work with the Fritz biographies on Patrick Henry, Benjamin Franklin, John Hancock, King George III, or Christopher Columbus.

3. At the end of *Why Don't You Get a Horse, Sam Adams?*, Fritz has given some notes with additional information. It could be useful to read those two pages and select items to share with students.

Kumin, Maxine. *The Microscope.*
Illustrated by Arnold Lobel. New York: Harper and Row, Publishers, 1984.

SUMMARY: Brief story, in verse, of Anton Leeuwenhoek and what he saw through his microscope.

GRADE LEVEL: Kindergarten through 2nd grade

CURRICULUM AREA: Science

OBJECTIVES: To introduce students to microscopes
To make students aware that there are real people behind scientific discoveries

ACTIVITY:
Materials: Microscope(s), slides, things to examine, art paper, crayons

1. Read Kumin's book to the class.

2. Discuss Leeuwenhoek with the class. Ask questions based on the content of the book that emphasize his character such as: What did Leeuwenhoek enjoy doing? What happened to his business? How did his neighbors feel about it? Why do you think he liked to do this?

3. Ask students to think of something they would like to look at under the microscope. (It may be necessary to give guidance here.)

4. Then ask students to make a picture of what they think it will look like. Have them label and sign these "before" pictures.

5. Tell students they will have a chance to look at their items in a microscope and then will be asked to draw what they see. Discuss with students the items to be examined. Discuss how students should behave around the microscope and how to look through it.

6. After students have examined their item, they will draw the "after" picture. Discuss with students the differences between what they actually saw and what they predicted they would see. Display the picture pairs.

7. Students should have a chance to observe, discuss, and ask questions about other minute items.

8. Discuss why microscopes are important and how they help us learn.

CONSIDERATIONS:
1. It may be advisable for students not to change slides and adjust the microscope, but only look through it. If so, volunteers or classroom aids could be assigned to change and adjust slides as children come to look. Or, the microscope could be set up with one slide, and then changed on a daily basis.

2. If several microscopes are available, this would work as a whole-class activity with the children divided into groups. Otherwise, it may be best to set up a learning center.

3. Experience with a microscope is preferred, but it would be possible to do this activity without a microscope *if* good photographs of protozoa, amoebas, and so on are available.

Nhuong, Huynh Quang. *The Land I Lost: Adventures of a Boy in Vietnam.*
New York: Harper and Row Publishers, 1982.

SUMMARY: The author shares his personal memories of daily life as he grew up in the central highlands of Vietnam. This well-written account will capture the interest and imagination of all.

GRADE LEVEL: 3rd through 6th grades

CURRICULUM AREA: Social Studies; Creative Writing; Multicultural Appreciation

OBJECTIVES: To increase student appreciation for other ways of life
To give students an opportunity to practice creative writing

ACTIVITY:
Materials: Paper, pencils

1. Read all or part of Nhuong's book. If only one chapter is used, it can be read at one time. If the whole book is shared, it may take several days.

2. After reading, students may wish to discuss the book.

3. Ask students to pretend they are writing a letter to Nhuong. They should select some aspect of their own life to explain to him, some incident or tradition, or some part of their life that they would want to share with someone from another culture.

4. Share or discuss student work.

CONSIDERATIONS:
1. The teacher may wish to collect these writings in a notebook in the classroom for parents' night.

2. Some students may wish to share their letters with the class.

Rosenberg, Maxine B. *Making a New Home in America.*
New York: Lothrop, Lee and Shepard Books, 1976.

SUMMARY: Jiro, Carmen, Daisely, and Farah share their experiences and feelings as they adjust to life in the United States.

GRADE LEVEL: 2nd through 4th grades

CURRICULUM AREA: Social Studies; Multicultural Appreciation

OBJECTIVES: To make students aware of some of the difficulties and advantages of moving

To make students aware of local examples of immigration

ACTIVITY:

Materials: Guest speaker or speakers

1. Share Rosenberg's book with students.

2. Discuss with the class some of the points made in the book about the feelings Jiro, Carmen, Daisely, and Farah had about moving and their experiences in the United States.

3. Work with the class to develop a list of questions they might like to ask someone who recently moved to the local area. For example: What do you like best here? What did you like best in your old home? What is different here? What do you miss most?

4. Tell students a guest speaker who has moved to the area from another country will be coming to visit with the class. (Students may be able to help identify potential speakers.)

5. When the guest speaker comes, he or she should talk about his or her experiences after moving to the area. Realia, props, pictures, or slides would be nice. Students might ask the questions formulated in step 3.

6. Students should write thank you notes to the speaker.

CONSIDERATIONS:

1. This activity presents a good opportunity to emphasize that books can tell about real people (biography).

2. If there is no one available who has recently moved from another country, consider asking someone who has moved to your area from another part of the United States, or asking someone from the United States who has lived in another country.

3. A tape recording or videotape might be useful if the person cannot come to the classroom.

"Good Read" Books

Some nonfiction titles are so well written that they can be judged as having literary merit. Recognition of such quality writing can be seen in some of the awards and prizes given children's books. The American Library Association supervises the annual awarding of the Newbery medal for the most distinguished contribution to American literature for children published in the preceding year. In judging the eligible titles, the emphasis is on the quality of the writing and the award is given to an *author*. Some nonfiction titles have been recognized in this way. Russell Freedman won the 1988 Newbery medal for *Lincoln: A Photobiography; Sugaring Time* by Kathryn Lasky was a Newbery honor book in 1984.

As with all nonfiction, a "good read" should be accurate, authoritative, current, and unbiased. Furthermore, it must be well written. This is a characteristic that is hard to quantify and define, but somewhat easier to recognize. The author's style, word choice, and enthusiasm for his or her topic work together to create a book that intrigues and entertains the reader. The topics can vary widely, from a biography of Lincoln that presents new aspects of the familiar man to a chance to share the experience of tapping maple trees and making maple syrup to a humorous exploration of quicksand.

Such well-written books encourage readers to explore new topics and can help to promote the fun of reading. Quality nonfiction can tempt fiction readers to try something different. And, in addition to being entertaining, the books are informative. Therefore, the reader is being presented with facts, theories, or ideas that conceivably can be transferred to other areas.

Sometimes nonfiction titles are underused. As adults, we frequently tend to think of fiction reading as recreational. Well-written, entertaining informational books can help to expand student horizons and keep readers interested in nonfiction titles. Fortunately, a number of authors such as Freedman, Lauber, and Lasky produce quality nonfiction titles that are "good reads."

de Paola, Tomie. *The Quicksand Book.*
New York: Holiday House, 1977.

SUMMARY: While Jungle Girl slowly sinks, Jungle Boy discusses the nature of quicksand and rescue procedures.

GRADE LEVEL: Kindergarten through 2nd grade

CURRICULUM AREA: Science; Scientific Method

OBJECTIVES: To teach students about quicksand
To show students the connection between books and science activities they suggest

ACTIVITY:
Materials: Bucket or pail with a hole in the bottom, a hose, sand, waterproof tape or putty, rocks, other heavy objects—some that will sink and some that won't

1.   Share the book with the children. It is a good title to read aloud.

2.   Do the activity detailed on the last page. If possible, work with children in small groups (four or five students per group) so all children can see what is happening.

3.   This opportunity could be used to help students explore scientific method. Have students suggest different objects (of different weights and different surface areas) to place on the quicksand. Also, vary the force of the water. Discuss results with students. Ask students what they think will happen and why. Then try it, discuss the results, and repeat the procedure with the next object.

CONSIDERATIONS:
1.   Not all students are ready to learn strictly from books. This activity gives them concrete experiences to build on.

2.   It may be advisable to do the experiment outdoors.

Freedman, Russell. *Children of the Wild West.*
New York: Clarion Book, 1983.

SUMMARY: Freedman details the lives of children in the west from 1840 to the early 1900s. Profusely illustrated with photographs.

GRADE LEVEL: 4th and 5th grades

CURRICULUM AREA: U.S. History; Creative Dramatics

OBJECTIVES: To increase student knowledge of the American frontier and the realities of daily life
To provide an opportunity for creative dramatics

ACTIVITY:

1. This activity is proposed as a follow-up to instruction on the American West.

2. Introduce Freedman's book to the class. Briefly summarize its content, emphasizing its detailed information about children.

3. Tell students the book will be available in the classroom. Have students pick an area they are interested in, such as attending school or crossing the plains in a covered wagon. Using the book, students should read about the area selected and study the accompanying pictures.

4. Next, have students pretend they are children in the American West. Using the information from Freedman's book, students should prepare a brief oral presentation (two to three minutes) about a typical incident in their lives on the frontier. While the content should be based on fact, it would be appropriate to include thoughts, feelings, or other details to bring to life the assumed personality.

5. Give students an opportunity to present their characters to the class.

CONSIDERATIONS:

1. Students can use the library media center for additional research on their topic.

2. This unit could correlate nicely with the *Little House* books of Laura Ingalls Wilder.

3. It may be appropriate to make an audiotape of student performances. Videotape is also a possibility, but this could necessitate costuming.

4. This activity could involve the whole class, or it would work as an extra-credit or supplementary activity. It could be appropriate for some students to work in pairs.

Giblin, James Cross. *Chimney Sweeps: Yesterday and Today.*
New York: Thomas Y. Crowell, 1982.

SUMMARY: A concise history of chimney sweeps from the 1400s to today.

GRADE LEVEL: 3rd and 4th grades

CURRICULUM AREA: History; Social Studies; Reality versus Movie Version of History

OBJECTIVES: To increase student knowledge of life in the 1700s

To make students aware of the role and function of chimney sweeps

To help students recognize the differences between the film version of chimney sweeps and the way it really was

ACTIVITY:

Materials: Recording of the chimney sweep's song from the Walt Disney's *Mary Poppins*, poster board or transparencies, appropriate marking pens

1. Play the chimney sweep's song for the students. If students don't know the role of the chimney sweep in Disney's movie, briefly summarize and explain the part to them. Then lead a discussion about what students think chimney sweeps do, whether they like their work, whether students would like to be chimney sweeps, and so forth.

2. Explain that in the 1700s young children were chimney sweeps. If the earlier discussion didn't include some negative aspects of working as chimney sweeps have students develop these now.

3. Then read chapter 5, "A Climbing Boy's Day," from Giblin's book.

4. Divide the class into groups. Each group will write three to five interview questions, such as: Who are you? Where do you work as a chimney sweep? Then they will write two answers, one for the Disney sweep and one for the Giblin sweep. Also, have the group try to explain why the Disney version is so different from Giblin's book.

5. Have each group share all or part of their interviews with the class. Posters or transparencies may be used. Or, three children may play the roles of the interviewer and two sweeps.

6. Have students discuss and try to explain the discrepancies in the two portrayals of sweeps.

7. Explain why chimney sweeps are needed and their role in preventing fires.

8. Have some or all students find out about chimney sweeps today. The school library media specialist may be able to help locate pictures and recent articles. This information should be shared briefly with the class.

CONSIDERATIONS:

1. This activity could work well with a study of energy and why people are burning wood and coal to help cut the cost of heating bills. It also could be part of a study on fire safety.

2. Information needed about the history of chimney sweeps and their role in preventing fires is contained in Giblin's book.

3. It may be appropriate to invite a chimney sweep or fireman to be a guest speaker in the classroom.

Lasky, Kathryn. *Sugaring Time.*
Photographs by Christopher G. Knight. New York: Macmillan Publishing Company, Inc., 1983.

SUMMARY: As spring comes to Vermont, the Laceys tap their maple trees and make maple syrup. Lasky's poetic language details the procedure.

GRADE LEVEL: 5th and 6th grades

CURRICULUM AREA: Social Studies; Language Arts; Applying Information

OBJECTIVES: To give students insight into a specialized part of American life
To teach students how to plan and execute a video production
To expose students to good informational writing

ACTIVITY:
Materials: Video camera, videotape, tagboard, felt tip pens, studio or place to film

1. Share Lasky's book with the class. All or part of the book could be read aloud. Or, students could be required to read the book while it is kept in the classroom.

2. Discuss the book with students. Stress Lasky's use of language and the way setting and mood are conveyed in the book.

3. Tell students they will be making a videotape based on the book. Each segment of the tape will feature a character from the book reflecting on what sugaring time means to him or her as an individual.

4. Divide the class into groups. Each group will explore the feelings of an assigned character, select one member to be the actor, and write their script. (It can be from one to five minutes in length. Students should practice and time their segments. Teachers can decide on the time allotments.) Scripts should show awareness of and appreciation for Lasky's use of language.

5. Characters can be chosen from the following list:

    Alice Lacey (mother)   Jumping Jack (Belgian workhorse)*

    Don Lacey (father)   Tommy (Belgian workhorse)*

    Jonathan Lacey (son, 8)   The dog*

    Angie Lacey (daughter, 6)   The maple tree*

    Jeremy Lacey (son, 3)   The maple sap*

    Betty Brown (grandmother)

    *Nonhuman characters may wish to speak through a human "friend"

6. After scripts are ready, plan the videotaping. An introduction and perhaps a narrator, need to be considered. Decide on: an order for characters to speak; scenery or a backdrop; simple costuming; and titles and credits. This work may be done as a whole class or in groups.

7. Put together a storyboard that details how the videotape will be shot. Include times, camera angles, and so forth.

8. Assign students to camera operation, cue cards, lighting, staging crews, directing, acting, and similar roles.

9. Shoot the videotape. Then play it back for class enjoyment.

CONSIDERATIONS:
1. You may wish to share the videotape with parents, teachers, or other classes.

2. It is possible to do this activity using slides and an audiotape to produce a sound/slide show.

3. To stress comprehension, students could use Lasky's book and write step-by-step directions for making maple syrup.

Lauber, Patricia. *Tales Mummies Tell.*
New York: Thomas Y. Crowell, 1985.

SUMMARY: From an intriguingly detailed discussion of a baby mammoth frozen near the Arctic Circle, Lauber goes on to explore different kinds of mummies and what scientists can learn from them about different civilizations.

GRADE LEVEL: 5th and 6th grades

CURRICULUM AREA: History; Science; Art; Evaluating Information

OBJECTIVES: To increase student knowledge about mummies and what they teach us
To give students an opportunity to identify most pertinent points in information they gather
To provide students an opportunity to plan and create a bulletin board

ACTIVITY:
Materials: Bulletin board supplies, colored construction paper, felt tip pens, scissors, lettering guides (if pictures are to be used, students should either draw or xerox them, *not* cut them out of books)

1. Introduce the topic of mummies to the students. Tell them they will be working in groups and each group will do a bulletin board.

2. Divide the students into groups. Each group will work with a different kind of mummy. Several categories are listed below:

- Mummies created by freezing (animal and/or human)
- Egyptian mummies (animal and/or human)
- Mummies formed in caves
- Mummies formed in fluid that kills bacteria
- Peruvian mummies
- Mummies in peat bogs

3. Students in each group should research their own type of mummy. Lauber's book contains excellent information and her bibliography gives additional sources of information. Students can also use the school library media center or public library for further information.

4. Students need to plan the bulletin board carefully before starting to work on it. They will need to decide which information will be included on the bulletin board. This gives them a chance to judge the value of the information found and identify the most important points since they must decide what must be included to explain their type of mummy when the amount of room is very limited. Also, they can decide which information can be conveyed visually (and in what form) and where words are needed. The bulletin boards should be accurate, concise, informative, appealing, and pique the interest of other students.

5. Have students actually make and set up the bulletin boards.

CONSIDERATIONS:
1. If enough bulletin board space is not available in the classroom, other sites in the school could be considered such as the school library media center.

2. It would be possible to use large sheets of butcher paper instead of bulletin boards, but actual bulletin boards would allow more flexibility in terms of the materials used.

Macaulay, David. *City: A Story of Roman Planning and Construction.*
Boston: Houghton Mifflin Company, 1974.

SUMMARY: Macaulay details the planning, engineering, and building of Verbonia, an imaginary Roman city started in 26 B.C.

GRADE LEVEL: 5th and 6th grades

CURRICULUM AREA: History; Library Skills; Evaluating Information

OBJECTIVES: To give students information about Roman cities
To increase student understanding of indexes

ACTIVITY:
Materials: Index cards

1.   Discuss with students the function of an index. It may be useful to have examples. Students may wish to share their personal experiences. Emphasize that an index should help a reader go directly to specific information in the book.

2.   Introduce the students to Macaulay's work. Explain it does not have an index and that the class will construct one. Ask students to brainstorm about some things they may do to make the job easier, or problems they may encounter. Be sure students know about cross references, "see" and "see also" entries, and the reverse order used for some terms in indexes, such as Clearly, Beverly.

3.   Divide the students into groups and assign each group certain pages to index. Each group should have a recorder who will keep track of procedures used, problems encountered, and decisions made as the group works.

4.   If students work with index cards, it will be easier to shuffle and rearrange the cards.

5.   When students have finished their section, they should compile a list of rules they followed and a brief set of tips for future indexers based on what worked and what did not.

6.   Lead a class discussion based on student lists from step 5. If possible, students should reach a consensus on the list of rules and the list of tips.

7.   After all groups have finished, one group or volunteers can use the index cards to create and type one index. They should check to ensure all references to the same things use the same terminology. Also, in some cases they may need to make a value judgment about the best term to use.

CONSIDERATIONS:
1.   This activity can be done for any information book without an index.

2.   If microcomputers are available, students could create and shuffle the index on the computer.

St. George, Judith. *The Brooklyn Bridge: They Said It Couldn't Be Built.*
New York: G. P. Putnam's Sons, 1982.

SUMMARY: Story of the people and processes involved in building the Brooklyn Bridge in the late 1800s.

GRADE LEVEL: 4th through 6th grades

CURRICULUM AREA: History; Creative Writing; Critical Thinking

OBJECTIVES: To show students that history can be fascinating and fun
To give students a chance to express themselves in writing

ACTIVITY:
Materials: Construction paper or poster board, crayons or felt tip pens

1. Set up a learning center containing St. George's book and the materials listed above in the classroom or school library media center. Prepare a bulletin board for display of student work.

2. Introduce students to the learning center, to St. George's book, and to the Brooklyn Bridge. It may also be necessary to introduce them to "Ripley's Believe It Or Not." Some examples would be useful.

3. The learning center will be available to students during free time.

4. Students will browse through the learning center or read the book by St. George. They should pick a "stranger-than-fiction" episode that appeals to them, and then create a "believe it or not" panel in words and drawings. Have students sign their work.

5. As students work on this project, they will create a bulletin board on the Brooklyn Bridge.

6. Discuss with students the idea of sensationalism as it applies to everyday things such as television programs or *The National Enquirer*. (The true facts emphasized in student work should provide examples that are both pertinent and familiar.) What is the purpose of sensationalism? Why do people or publications use it? How can readers recognize it? How can readers check on the truth of articles that seem to use sensationalism? Were students themselves tempted to sensationalize their panel on the Brooklyn Bridge?

CONSIDERATIONS:
1. If there is a lot of student response, it may be necessary to rotate the work displayed on the bulletin board.

2. For the final discussion, teachers may wish to have students watch a particular television show that deliberately seems to use sensationalism. Then other sources could be used for additional information. This would reverse the technique used in the learning center and provide additional material for discussion.

Appendix A:
Selected Sources

Booklist and Reference Books Bulletin. Chicago: American Library Association. Twice monthly September through June, monthly July and August.

Contains reviews of current recommended children's books, including nonfiction. Occasional special bibliographies may also feature nonfiction titles.

Carr, Jo, comp. *Beyond Fact: Nonfiction for Children and Young People*. Chicago: American Library Association, 1982.

Carr has collected a series of articles about nonfiction for children. Separate chapters on science, history, and biography.

Fisher, Margery. *Matters of Fact: Aspects of Nonfiction for Children*. New York: Thomas Y. Crowell, 1972.

An exploration of various types and facets of nonfiction for children. Includes a thought-provoking section on biography.

Horn Book Magazine. Boston: The Horn Book, Inc. Six issues a year.

Contains articles about literature for children and young adults and reviews of recommended titles. Nonfiction is included. Emphasis is on literary aspects.

Huck, Charlotte S., Susan Helper, and Janet Hickman. *Children's Literature in the Elementary School*. 4th edition. New York: Holt, Rinehart and Winston, 1987.

A general textbook on children's literature with a chapter on information books and using them in the classroom. Also includes a section on children's biography. Extensive lists of recommended titles are given.

Kobrin, Beverly. *Eyeopeners! How to Choose and Use Children's Books about Real People, Places, and Things*. New York: Penguin Books, 1988.

Discusses and reviews over 500 nonfiction books for children, with tips for their use. Includes suggestions to guide readers in selection of additional nonfiction books to use with students.

———. *The Kobrin Letter: Concerning Children's Books about Real People, Places, and Things*. Palo Alto, Calif.: Beverly Kobrin. Eight issues per year.

This journal reviews and recommends nonfiction for children.

Learning. Springhouse, Pa.: Springhouse Corporation. Nine issues per year.

Contains articles and teaching ideas pertinent to elementary and middle school teachers. Often gives bibliographies of suggested books to use with students, including nonfiction titles.

"Notable Children's Trade Books in the Field of Social Studies." In *Social Education*. Washington, D.C.: National Council for the Social Studies. Listed annually.

This bibliography lists fiction and nonfiction children's titles pertinent to social studies published in the previous year. All titles are deemed to be notable. (See appendix B.)

O'Connell, S. M., V. J. Montengro, and K. Wolf, eds. *The Best Science Books and A-V Materials for Children*. Washington, D.C.: American Association for the Advancement of Science, 1989.

Lists over 800 books and 400 films, videos, and filmstrips that were recommended in *Science Books and Films* (see below) between 1982 and 1988.

"Outstanding Science Trade Books for Children." In *Science and Children*. Washington, D.C.: National Science Teachers Association. Listed annually.

This list annually identifies the most outstanding science books published during the previous year using such criteria as accuracy, readability, and quality of the format. (See appendix B.)

School Library Journal. New York: A. Cahners/R. R. Bowker. Monthly.

Includes articles pertinent to children's literature and reviews of both recommended and not recommended books and audiovisual materials for children. Nonfiction titles are covered, too.

Science and Children. Washington, D.C.: National Science Teachers Association. Eight issues annually.

Includes articles and reviews of interest to elementary and middle school science teachers.

Science Books and Films. Washington, D.C.: American Association for the Advancement of Science. Five issues a year.

Critical reviews of all types of science materials — books, films, filmstrips, videos — in all areas of science and mathematics. Includes materials for children.

Social Education. Washington, D.C.: National Council for the Social Studies. Seven issues annually.

Articles and reviews of interest to those who teach social studies. Includes both fiction and nonfiction.

Appendix B:
Selected 1989 Titles from Science and Social Studies Lists

Each year, the National Council for the Social Studies and the National Science Teachers Association identify new books in their respective fields which are considered to be notable or outstanding titles. These lists, along with the criteria and procedures used to determine which books will be included, are published in *Social Education* and *Science and Children*. Selected social studies titles (from the April/May 1990 *Social Education*) and science titles (from the March 1990 *Science and Children*) are listed here. All titles were published in 1989.

Aaseng, Nathan. *The Fortunate Fortunes*. Lerner.

Adair, Gene. *George Washington Carver*. Chelsea House.

Adler, David A. *A Picture Book of Martin Luther King, Jr.* Holiday House.

Adler, David A. *We Remember the Holocaust*. Holt.

Agard, John. *The Calypso Alphabet*. Holt.

Aliki. *The King's Day: Louis XIV of France*. Crowell.

Anderson, Joan. *The American Family Farm*. Harcourt, Brace, Jovanovich.

Anderson, Joan. *Spanish Pioneers of the Southwest*. Lodestar.

Anno, Mitsumasa. *Anno's Math Games II*. Philomel.

Ardley, Neil. *Music*. Knopf.

Arnold, Caroline. *Cheetah*. Morrow.

Arnold, Caroline. *Dinosaur Mountain: Graveyard of the Past*. Clarion.

Arnold, Caroline. *Hippo*. Morrow.

Arnold, Caroline. *Tule Elk*. Carolrhoda.

Arnosky, Jim. *Come Out, Muskrats*. Lothrop.

Arnosky, Jim. *In the Forest: A Portfolio of Paintings*. Lothrop.

Arthur, Alex. *Shell*. Knopf.

Ashabranner, Brent. *Born to the Land: An American Portrait*. Putnam.

Ashabranner, Melissa, and Brent Ashabranner. *Counting America: The Story of the United States Census*. Putnam.

Bannan, Jan Gumprech. *Sand Dunes*. Carolrhoda.

Bare, Colleen Stanley. *Never Kiss an Alligator!* Cobblehill.

Barton, Byron. *Dinosaurs, Dinosaurs*. Crowell.

Bash, Barbara. *Desert Giant: The World of the Saguaro Cactus*. Little Brown/ Sierra Club.

Berger, Melvin. *The Science of Music*. Crowell.

Berger, Melvin. *Switch On, Switch Off*. Crowell.

Billings, Charlene W. *Grace Hopper: Navy Admiral and Computer Pioneer*. Enslow.

Branley, Franklyn M. *What Happened to the Dinosaurs?* Crowell.

Brenner, Barbara, and May Garelick. *Two Orphan Cubs*. Walker.

Brownstone, David M. *Natural Wonders of America*. Atheneum.

Bruun, Ruth Dowling, and Bertel Bruun. *The Brain: What It Is, What It Does*. Greenwillow.

Burnie, David. *Plant*. Knopf.

Burton, Jane. *Animals Keeping Cool*. Random House.

A Children's Chorus. Dutton.

Clifford, Mary Louise. *The Land and People of Afghanistan*. Lippincott.

Cobb, Vicki. *Writing It Down*. Lippincott.

Coldrey, Jennifer. *Strawberry*. Silver Burdett.

Connolly, Peter. *Tiberius Claudius Maximus: The Cavalryman*. Oxford.

Crampton, William. *Flag*. Knopf.

Crofford, Emily. *Healing Warrior: A Story about Sister Elizabeth Kenny*. Carolrhoda.

Dewey, Jennifer Owings. *Birds of Antarctica: The Wandering Albatross*. Little, Brown.

Dewey, Jennifer Owings. *Can You Find Me? A Book about Animal Camouflage*. Scholastic.

Dorros, Arthur. *Feel the Wind*. Crowell.

Dunrea, Olivier. *Deep Down Underground*. Macmillan.

Erlich, Amy. *The Story of Hanukkah*. Dial.

Faber, Doris, and Harold Faber. *The Birth of a Nation: The Early Years of the United States*. Scribner.

Facklam, Margery. *Disturb: The Mysteries of Animal Hibernation and Sleep*. Little Brown/Sierra Club.

Facklam, Margery. *Partners for Life: The Mysteries of Animal Symbiosis*. Little Brown/Sierra Club.

Ferris, Jer. *Arctic Explorer: The Story of Matthew Henson*. Fifth Avenue Editions.

Finkelstein, Norman H. *The Other 1492: Jewish Settlement in the New World*. Scribner.

Fischer-Nagel, Heiderose, and Andreas Fischer-Nagel. *Ant Colony*.

Fisher, Leonard Everett. *The Wailing Wall*. Macmillan.

Fisher, Leonard Everett. *The White House*. Holiday House.

Fisher, Maxine P. *Women in the Third World*. Watts.

Fleming, Thomas. *Behind the Headlines: The Story of American Newspapers*. Walker.

Florian, Douglas. *Nature Walk*. Greenwillow Books.

Florian, Douglas. *Turtle Day*. Crowell.

Forsyth, Adrian. *Journey through a Tropical Jungle*. Simon and Schuster.

Fritz, Jean. *The Great Little Madison*. Putnam.

Gallant, Roy A. *Ancient Indians: The First Americans*. Enslow.

Gallant, Roy A. *Before the Sun Dies: The Story of Evolution*. Macmillan.

George, William T. *Box Turtle at Long Pond*. Greenwillow.

Gibbons, Gail. *Marge's Diner*. Crowell.

Goodall, Jane. *The Chimpanzee Family Book*. Picture Book Studio.

Greenberg, Harvey R. *Emotional Illness in Your Family: Helping Your Relative, Helping Yourself*. Macmillan.

Haban, Rita D. *How Proudly They Wave: Flags of the Fifty States*. Lerner.

Harrar, George, and Linda Harrar. *Signs of the Apes, Songs of the Whales: Adventures in Human-Animal Communication*. Simon and Schuster.

Harris, Jonathan. *The Land and People of France*. Lippincott.

Hausherr, Rosmarie. *Children and the AIDS Virus: A Book for Children, Parents, and Teachers*. Clarion.

Herberman, Ethan. *The City Kid's Field Guide*. Simon and Schuster.

Horenstein, Henry. *Sam Goes Trucking*. Houghton.

Hoxie, Frederick E. *The Crow*. Chelsea House.

Hyde, Margaret O. *The Homeless: Profiling the Problem*. Enslow.

Isberg, Emily. *Peak Performance: Sports, Science, and the Body in Action*. Simon and Schuster.

Jenness, Aylette, and Alice Rivers. *In Two Worlds: A Yup'ik Eskimo Family*. Houghton.

Johnson, Rebecca L. *The Secret Language: Pheromones in the Animal World*. Lerner.

Johnson, Sylvia A. *Elephant Seals*. Lerner.

Jurmain, Suzanne. *Once upon a Horse: A History of Horses—and How They Shaped Our History*. Lothrop.

Katz, William Loren, and Marc Crawford. *The Lincoln Brigade: A Picture History*. Atheneum.

Kerby, Mona. *Asthma*. Watts.

Kerby, Mona. *Cockroaches*. Watts.

Krementz, Jill. *How It Feels to Fight for Your Life*. Joy Street.

Krupp, E. C. *The Big Dipper and You*. Morrow.

Kudlinski, Kathleen. *Helen Keller: A Light for the Blind*. Viking.

Lacey, Elizabeth A. *The Complete Frog: A Guide for the Very Young Naturalist*. Lacey.

Lauber, Patricia. *The News about Dinosaurs*. Bradbury.

Lauber, Patricia. *Voyagers from Space: Meteors and Meteorites*. Crowell.

Lawson, Don. *The Abraham Lincoln Brigade: Americans Fighting Fascism in the Spanish Civil War*. Crowell.

Lavies, Bianca. *Lily Pad Pond*. Dutton.

Lerner, Carol. *Plant Families*. Morrow.

Leroi-Gourham, Andre. *The Hunters of Prehistory*. Atheneum.

Lyon, George Ella. *A B CEDAR: An Alphabet of Trees*. Orchard.

MacCarthy, Patricia. *Animals Galore!* Dial.

Major, John S. *The Land and People of China*. Lippincott.

Mallory, Kenneth, and Andrea Conley. *Rescue of the Stranded Whales*. Simon and Schuster.

Maren, Michael. *The Land and People of Kenya*. Lippincott.

Marzollo, Jean. *Getting Your Period: A Book about Menstruation*. Dial.

Matthews, Downs. *Polar Bear Cubs*. Simon and Schuster.

Maurer, Richard. *Junk in Space*. Simon and Schuster.

McKissack, Patricia C. *Jesse Jackson: A Biography*. Scholastic.

McKissack, Patricia, and Frederick McKissack. *A Long Hard Journey: The Story of the Pullman Porter*. Walker.

McLaughlin, Molly. *Dragonflies*. Walker.

Meltzer, Milton. *American Politics: How It Really Works*. Morrow.

Meltzer, Milton. *Voices from the Civil War: A Documentary History of the Great American Conflict*. Crowell.

Merriman, Nick. *Early Humans*. Knopf.

Michels, Tilde. *At the Frog Pond*. Lippincott.

Morris, Ann. *Bread, Bread, Bread*. Lothrop.

Munro, Roxie. *Blimps*. Dutton.

Munro, Roxie. *The Inside-Outside Book of London*. Dutton.

Murphy, Jim. *The Call of the Wolves*. Scholastic.

National Geographic Society. *Adventures in Your National Parks*. National Geographic.

Neimark, Anne E. *Che: Latin America's Legendary Guerilla Leader*. Lippincott.

National Wildlife Federation. *Endangered Animals*. National Wildlife Federation.

Norman, David, and Angela Milner. *Dinosaur*. Knopf.

Nourse, Alan E. *Your Immune System*. Watts.

Oakes, Catherine. *Exploring the Past: The Middle Ages*. Gulliver.

Parker, Steve. *Mammal*. Knopf.

Parker, Steve. *Seashore*. Knopf.

Parnall, Peter. *Quiet*. Morrow.

Patent, Dorothy Henshaw. *Humpback Whales*. Holiday House.

Patent, Dorothy Henshaw. *Looking at Dolphins and Porpoises*. Holiday House.

Patent, Dorothy Henshaw. *Wild Turkey, Tame Turkey*. Clarion.

Perl, Lila. *The Great Ancestor Hunt: The Fun of Finding Out Who You Are.* Clarion.

Peters, David. *A Gallery of Dinosaurs and Other Early Reptiles.* Knopf.

Pringle, Laurence. *The Animal Rights Controversy.* Harcourt, Brace, Jovanovich.

Pringle, Laurence. *Nuclear Energy: Troubled Past, Uncertain Future.* Macmillan.

Ray, Delia. *Gold: The Klondike Adventure.* Lodestar.

Reed, Don C. *The Dolphins and Me.* Little Brown/Sierra Club.

Riha, Susanne. *Animals in Winter.* Carolrhoda.

Roop, Peter, and Connie Roop. *Seasons of the Cranes.* Walker.

Rosenblum, Richard. *The Old Synagogue.* Jewish Publication Society.

Ryden, Hope. *Wild Animals of Africa ABC.* Lodestar.

Ryder, Joanne. *Where Butterflies Grow.* Lodestar.

Sancha, Sheila. *Walter Dragun's Town: Crafts and Trade in the Middle Ages.* Crowell.

Sattler, Helen Roney. *The Book of Eagles.* Lothrop.

Sattler, Helen Roney. *Tyrannosaurus Rex and Its Kin: The Mesozoic Monsters.* Lothrop.

Schnieper, Claudia. *Amazing Spiders.* Carolrhoda.

Schnieper, Claudia. *Chameleons.* Carolrhoda.

Schwartz, David M. *If You Made a Million.* Lothrop.

Schwartz, Lynne Sharon. *The Four Questions.* Dial.

Selsam, Millicent, and Joyce Hunt. *Keep Looking!* Macmillan.

Silverstein, Alvin, and Virginia Silverstein. *Glasses and Contact Lenses: Your Guide to Eyes, Eyewear, and Eye Care.* Lippincott.

Simon, Seymour. *Whales.* Crowell.

Singer, Marilyn. *Turtle in July.* Macmillan.

Smith, Norman F., and Douglas W. Smith. *Simulators*. Watts.

Srogi, LeeAnn. *Start Collecting Rocks and Minerals*. Running Press.

St. George, Judith. *Panama Canal: Gateway to the World*. Putnam.

Sussman, Susan, and Robert James. *Big Friend, Little Friend: A Book about Symbiosis*. Houghton.

Tanenhaus, Sam. *Louis Armstrong*. Chelsea House.

Turner, Dorothy. *Potatoes*. Carolrhoda.

Turner, Glennette Tilley. *Take a Walk in Their Shoes*. Cobblehill.

Ventura, Piero. *Michaelangelo's World*. Putnam.

Waters, Kate. *Sarah Morton's Day: A Day in the Life of a Pilgrim Girl*. Scholastic.

Whipple, Laura. *Eric Carle's Animals, Animals*. Philomel.

White, Sandra Verrill. *Sterling: The Rescue of a Baby Harbor Seal*. Crown.

Whitfield, Philip. *Can the Whales Be Saved? Questions about the Natural World and the Threats to Its Survival Answered by the National History Museum*. Viking.

Yoshida, Toshi. *Young Lions*. Philomel.

Zubrowski, Bernie. *Tops: Building and Experimenting with Spinning Toys*. Morrow.

Grade Level Index

Subject/Activity Index